Alfred Holborn

The Bible

The Sunday School Text-Book

Alfred Holborn

The Bible
The Sunday School Text-Book

ISBN/EAN: 9783337172855

Printed in Europe, USA, Canada, Australia, Japan

Cover: Foto ©Lupo / pixelio.de

More available books at **www.hansebooks.com**

NORMAL STUDIES FOR SUNDAY SCHOOL TEACHERS.

THE BIBLE:

THE SUNDAY SCHOOL TEXT-BOOK.

BY

ALFRED HOLBORN, M.A. LOND.

*PREPARED UNDER THE DIRECTION OF
THE INTERNATIONAL NORMAL COMMITTEE.*

BOSTON:
Congregational Sunday-School and Publishing Society,
CONGREGATIONAL HOUSE.

AMERICAN EDITION, COPYRIGHTED, 1885.

CONTENTS.

INTRODUCTORY LETTER ADDRESSED TO SUNDAY SCHOOL TEACHERS.

                                                                                                                                      PAGE

Origin and purpose of this book—Plan excludes the question of inspiration—Considerations pointing to a Divine origin of the Bible: (1) Its survival of all attempts to destroy it—and (2) all attempts to destroy belief in it—(3) Its vast circulation—(4) Its influence on modern literature—(5) Its influence on human life and character. The Bible a unity—A progressive revelation—How this Text-book should be studied vii

CHAPTER I.

ON THE EVIDENCES OF THE AUTHENTICITY AND GENUINENESS OF THE SACRED WRITINGS.

The evidence for the Old Testament based on that for the New. I. *New Testament.*—Pauline Epistles selected for a starting-point—(1) Internal evidence for these Epistles—General characteristics—Undesigned coincidences—Romans, Corinthians, and Galatians examined—(2) External testimony to the Pauline Epistles—(3) The Gospels and other books of the New Testament—Their contents corroborated by the Epistles—Internal evidence—Testimony of Papias, Justin, Irenæus, etc.—Comparison with Apocryphal Gospels. II. *Old Testament.*—Contents verified by profane history, etc.—Frequent quotation of the Old Testament by Christ—and by the evangelists and apostles—Interdependence of the Old Testament and the New 1

CHAPTER II.

ON THE FORMATION OF THE CANON: CHARACTERISTICS OF THE SEVERAL BOOKS.

Meaning of the word "canon." I. Canon of the Old Testament—Formed gradually—"The Law"—"The Prophets"—"The Writings"—Synod of Jamnia—The Canon of Josephus. II. Canon of the New Testament—Formed gradually—Earlier portion—Later additions—Persecution of Diocletian—Council of Carthage—Authority of Scripture not due to councils—Table from Dr. Charteris's "Canonicity." Summary of the contents and characteristics of the principal canonical books 25

CHAPTER III.

ON THE LANGUAGE AND STYLE OF SCRIPTURE: THE BIBLE A UNIQUE BOOK.

Language and style of Scripture vary in the different books—Nevertheless some common characteristics: 1. Dignity—2. Reference throughout to God and righteousness—2. Suppression of the personality of the writers—4. Impartiality and candour—5. Dramatic style—6. Simplicity and sobriety—7. Figurative speech—8. Parallelism—9. The Bible a unique book—Testimonies of Dr. Huxley, Sir Walter Scott, and Sir William Jones 50

CHAPTER IV.

ON THE STUDY OF SCRIPTURE WITH SPECIAL REFERENCE TO SUNDAY SCHOOL INSTRUCTION.

The teacher must know more than he teaches—1. The Bible to be studied as a book of human life—2. The progress of Divine revelation—In morality—Modes of worship—The idea of God—The doctrine of the future life—3. The Bible must be studied historically—Epitome of Bible history—4. Other studies necessary—5. Plan for the reading of Scripture—6. Preparation of the lesson—7. Scripture difficulties: (i.) Miracles—(ii.) Apparent contradiction in statements of fact—(iii.) Apparent contradiction in doctrine—(iv.) The bad actions of good men—(v.) Evil things apparently done with Divine approval—(vi.) The imprecatory Psalms—(vii.) Anthropomorphism and Anthropopathism—(viii.) Passages which offend our delicacy of taste 66

CHAPTER V.

ON THE MEANS OF RELIGIOUS INSTRUCTION, PUBLIC AND PRIVATE, UNDER THE OLD AND NEW TESTAMENTS, WITH EXAMPLES.

The information scanty and scattered—1. Parental instruction—2. Instruction by rites and symbols—3. Public reading of the Scriptures—4. Instruction by teachers divinely commissioned—The prophets—5. The schools of the prophets—6. The service of song—7. The synagogue—8. Schools—9. The Christian Church 95

CHAPTER VI.

ON THE TEACHING PROCESS, AS EXEMPLIFIED IN THE BIBLE: IN QUESTIONING, METAPHOR AND SIMILE, OBJECT ILLUSTRATION, PARABLE, AND PRACTICAL APPLICATION.

1. Questioning—Different forms answering different purposes—Christ's use of the art of questioning—2. Metaphor and simile—Defined and illustrated—Metaphors and similes of Scripture mostly drawn from natural objects—Examples from the writings of Paul and other apostles—3. Object illustration—In the Old Testament—In the Gospels—In the Epistles—4. The parable—Defined and distinguished from the fable—Parable of Nathan—Later prophets—Parables of our Lord— 5. Practical application—Need for this in teaching children—Instances in the Old Testament—In the discourses of Christ—In the Acts of the Apostles—In the Epistles 114

APPENDIX 133

INDEX 143

The other volumes of NORMAL STUDIES *now ready are as follows:* —

THE YOUNG TEACHER: An Elementary Handbook of Sunday-school Instruction. By WM. H. GROSER, B.Sc., with an Introduction by J. H. VINCENT, D.D. Price 75 cts.

CONTENTS. — I. The Sunday School, its Scope and Aims. — II. The Chief Qualifications of the Sunday-school Teacher. — III. Principles of Instruction, and their Relation to Bible Teaching. — IV. Methods of Instruction : their Use in Bible Teaching. — V. Bible Lessons, and How to Prepare Them. — VI. Class Teaching. — VII. Class Management. — VIII. Helps and Hinderances.

PRIMER OF CHRISTIAN EVIDENCE. By R. A. REDFORD, M.A., LL.B. Price 75 cts.

CONTENTS. — I. What Christianity is. — II. What the Credentials of Christianity are. — III. What Christianity is to the World. — IV. How Christian Evidences should be Studied. — V. How to Teach the Old Testament.

Address all orders to the CONGREGATIONAL SUNDAY SCHOOL AND PUBLISHING SOCIETY, *corner* BEACON AND SOMERSET STREETS, BOSTON.

Note to the American Edition.

No teachers have so strong reasons for desiring the highest skill as those who teach the Word of God. That their great aim is to induce their pupils to surrender their wills to the will of God, and to develop into moral and spiritual perfection those into whom the Holy Spirit has come to abide, only makes it more necessary that they should understand the principles and methods of instruction.

The last twenty-five years have witnessed great advances in knowledge of the art of teaching. Schools for training teachers are now provided at public expense in nearly all the States of the Union. New text-books are constantly being written on the subject; and new methods of applying the principles of instruction, and of developing the mental powers, are constantly being tested and described. The average Sunday-school teacher has not time for thorough and extended training in the art of teaching. He is busy in other callings. His work in the Sunday-school is voluntary; and his continuance in it is not secured by ordinary business obligations, but by the higher motive of service to his fellow-men for Christ's sake. The strength of these motives is determined by the activity of his spiritual life and his faith in God; and these are constantly in danger of being weakened from many causes. To set the standard of his qualifications too high is to discourage him altogether, and banish him from the school. The question, how much of this training should be insisted on as essential to his fitness for his work, is a most important one.

In the presence of some opposition and much more indifference, increasing efforts have been made, for several years, to furnish some sort of special training to Sunday-school teachers. In this movement Dr. J. H. Vincent has been from the first the acknowledged leader. Through his guidance, and for this purpose, the Chautauqua Sunday-School Assembly was organized ten years ago. A number of books have been written on the subject, of which many of the best have been either by his pen or under his direction. Summer Assemblies have multiplied, and have expanded beyond their original aim. Sunday-school teachers from all parts of the country have been made acquainted with each other, and have awakened in each other holier fervor and more exalted ideas of their mission by mutual intercourse.

Still, it is plain enough that the churches have not yet taken up the idea that this teacher-training is their business. Special efforts in the churches in this direction are the exception. Only a small proportion of them have any meetings for the purpose of studying how to teach. Theological seminaries have, as yet, no place in their curriculum for instructing students in the art of teaching teachers. The subject rarely finds a place in the programmes of church conferences or associations; and when it does, there are few who can so treat it as to kindle interest and furnish valuable information.

Yet the churches are sensitive to the necessity of special training for their *pastors*. They are slow to trust a company of a hundred or more to the care of one unprepared for his work. It is only natural to look in the near future for a similar demand for those to whose pastoral guidance companies of five and ten are entrusted. The leadership that was once confined to a few professional men has extended itself to a great multitude of laymen and women; and, surrounded as they are by the growing spirit of inquiry in regard to secular teaching, they will seek for at least a knowledge of the elementary principles of the art of teaching, as applied to the Sunday-school.

The issue of this series of text-books is one important step in this direction. The demand for them, expressed four years ago in the action of the Centenary Meeting in London, is much greater now than it was then. They will themselves create a greater interest, and lead to the preparation of other books in the same line. When the task of revising them was first committed to me, I intended making extensive changes. But a more thorough examination convinced me that this would be unjust to their authors, and I have contented myself with only such alterations as seemed necessary to adapt the books to American readers. I have added to the Primer of Christian Evidence a part of the excellent little treatise of Principal Benham on "How to Teach the Old Testament," because of its suggestive hints in the line of the course of lessons I have prepared for the second year of a course of normal study.

This course is another important step in the training of Sunday-school teachers. Taking these books as a basis, a series of lessons has been prepared, which, with the readings connected with them, may profitably occupy such time as the average teacher may be likely to be able to appropriate to such study for two years. Individuals in correspondence with the managers, and by the use of leaflets which will be furnished, may pursue the course alone. Classes of teachers under the guidance of pastors may undertake it with still greater advantage.*

Nearly all the larger Summer Assemblies have already adopted this course; and if those who study it through the year will come up to the Assemblies to meet competent teachers with such questions as they may wish to ask, listen to the lectures, and take part in the daily drill and examinations, they will so fit themselves for their work that they may reasonably expect a higher degree of success.

More than that, the meeting and intercourse of teachers of different religious denominations and from different sections of the country, in a fraternity organized on the basis of this common aim and study, will greatly promote the interests of the Sunday-school. I welcome with great joy this Christian fel-

---

* Any desiring further information concerning this Assembly Normal Union may address either myself or Rev. J. L. Hurlburt, D.D., 705 Broadway, New York.

lowship and the noble results it promises, and would gladly pray for the special gifts of the Holy Spirit for teaching His truth to each one who enters into it.

May these books help many fellow-workers to greater success in winning souls, and in informing them concerning the thoughts and will of God, and transforming them into the image of His dear Son.

A. E. Dunning.

Congregational House, Boston.

INTRODUCTORY LETTER.

Addressed to Sunday school Teachers, and especially to the Young Teachers for whom this book is more particularly designed.

My dear Friends,

This little work has been written at the request of the Committee of the Sunday School Union, in furtherance of a scheme drawn up by the International Normal Committee, which embraced representatives of the Sunday school work in America as well as Great Britain. Their desire was to afford you some guidance in the pursuance of a course of reading and study, which would enable you to discharge more efficiently the important duties you have undertaken. The scheme falls into three parts, of which the second relates to "the Bible as the Sunday school Text-book." You will, of course, understand that by "text-book" is meant not a book of texts, but a manual of instruction—a book to be used in class as the "text" upon which your teaching is to be the "commentary." Your aim goes beyond the mere teaching the contents of the Bible, however intelligently this may be done. Your aim is to "teach Christ"—to bring your scholars into personal and saving relations with the Redeemer of mankind, and to mould them in His likeness. But for this purpose the

Bible is indispensable as a text-book. It contains all we know of Jesus Christ, and of the way in which God prepared mankind for His coming. It is, therefore, your hand-book, which you will use as every good teacher uses the hand-book or class-book on any subject which he has to teach; first mastering its contents yourself, and gathering from all quarters information which will enable you to employ them most effectually for the main end you have in view.

The International Committee laid down the divisions of the subject, and though, in some respects, I should have preferred a different plan, I have thought it best, on the whole, to adhere to theirs in the headings of the following chapters, with only very slight modification. The first chapter will show you by what evidence the genuineness and authenticity of the several books is established; the second describes the gradual process of their collection into one volume, the Canon of Holy Scripture, and briefly indicates the contents and characteristics of its several parts; the third calls attention to some features in the language and style of Scripture which make this volume a unique book The International Committee have deemed it wise not to enter on the question of Inspiration, but I should like at the outset to lay before you some considerations which may strengthen your own faith in the Divine origin of the Bible, and provide you with a reply to such persons as would class this volume among the ordinary productions of the human intellect. These considerations do not require us to assume or discuss any particular theory of inspiration, but only to ponder certain undeniable facts connected with the history of the Book.

1. First of all, I would call your attention to the

remarkable way in which this Book has outlived all attempts to destroy it. When Antiochus Epiphanes conquered Palestine, 168 B.C., he determined to extirpate the Jewish religion, and commanded all copies of the Law to be burned, and every one found in possession of a copy to be put to death. In the year 303 of our era, the Emperor Diocletian issued a similar edict throughout the whole Roman Empire, with regard to the New Testament scriptures, which was carried into effect with the utmost rigour. The Roman Catholic Church, as you are well aware, made the most vigorous efforts, at the time of the Reformation, not, indeed, to destroy the sacred originals, but to destroy all copies of them in the language of the people; and in addition to these might be enumerated other attempts, more partial in their extent, to banish the volume of Holy Writ from the realm of literature. But, in spite of all these strenuous endeavours to destroy it, the Bible has survived, and not only survived, but multiplied to an extent utterly unparalleled in the case of any other book whatever.

2. Consider, again, the attempts made to destroy *belief* in the Bible—the vast number of books written to oppose its teaching, to invalidate its historical testimony, or to refute its claims to Divine authority. If we were to begin with the writings of its early opponents, Celsus and Porphyry, and gather together all such works as have appeared in succeeding centuries down to the present date, we should have enough to fill the shelves of a well-fitted library. "If all these books," says Professor Rogers, "were placed in one library, and this single volume set on a table in the midst of it, and a stranger were told that this book had drawn upon itself for its exposure, confutation,

and destruction this multitude of volumes, I imagine he would be inclined to say, 'Then, I presume this little Book was annihilated long ago; though how it could be needful to write a thousandth part so much for any such purpose, I cannot comprehend.' How surprised would he then be to learn that they were felt to be not *enough;* that similar works were being multiplied every day, and still to no purpose in disabusing mankind of this frenzy. He would learn, indeed, that so far from accomplishing their object, the new volumes are little more than necessary to replace those of this fruitful and yet fruitless literature which are continually sinking into oblivion."

3. And whilst this is the fate of the volumes written to "put down" the Bible, what is the fate of the Book itself? The demand for it goes on increasing from year to year. In 1881 the Revised Version of the New Testament was published. It was known beforehand that the alterations of the Authorised Version would not be very material. One might have thought that a slightly modified translation of an old book, the general contents of which were well known before, could not create a very large demand. But so intense is the interest which *this* old Book has awakened in itself, that the Oxford University Press *alone* received orders in *advance* for more than a million copies. When it was actually published, the demand for copies, both here and in America, exceeded the powers of the printing press to keep up with them. One newspaper in Chicago published the entire New Testament in its issue of May 22, 1881, the greater portion having been *transmitted from New York by telegraph.* How can the sceptic account for this extraordinary and universal eagerness to obtain copies of the New Version of this old book, if, as

he says, it has long since been proved to be in the main a collection of fictitious histories and fantastic dreamings!

Meanwhile, the Old Version goes on circulating at the rate of about *six million* copies a year. The issue of the British and Foreign Bible Society for 1882 was 2,964,636 copies; and after careful examination of the statistics kindly furnished to me by the secretaries of this and other societies, I calculate that about an equal number are supplied from all other societies and private publishing houses taken together. The largest proportion of these are in the English tongue, but it is worthy of special notice that the whole Bible, or considerable portions of it, have been translated into 298 languages and dialects, and these have found a welcome wherever they have come. Now, it would be vain for the sceptic to try to evade the force of these facts by saying, "It is easy enough to account for the numerous translations and extensive circulation of the Scriptures when there are large and wealthy societies formed for that express purpose"—because it is the *Bible itself that has called these societies into existence.* There has lately been formed a "Browning Society," for the purpose of promoting the study of the works of Robert Browning. Should the result be that the works of Robert Browning circulate at the rate of six millions a year in three hundred different languages, it will not in the least impair the tribute due to the author's genius to say that this result has been affected through the agency of a society which his own works created and inspired.

4. The same remark applies to the one other fact I would bring before your notice, viz. the enormous influence which the Bible has had on all modern literature; and the

vast amount which it has directly called into existence. It has permeated all the streams of poetic, æsthetic, philosophic, and even historical literature. Traces of the Bible are to be found on the pages of every author outside the realms of mere technical science; and the orator involuntarily quotes its phrases as the most forcible way of expressing his sentiments, and emphasizing his periods; while the books expressly written to expound the contents and enforce the teaching of this one volume, would form no insignificant proportion of the entire mass of literature of all kinds taken together. Twenty-one volumes of the Catalogue of the Library of the British Museum are devoted to the single heading, "Bible;" and yet these twenty-one volumes *by no means* embrace the titles of all the books in that library written about the Bible; many, probably the greater number, being classified under other headings, such as the author's name, etc. This is a unique phenomenon. The nearest approach to it is in the case of the works of Shakespeare, who has his name at the head of five and a quarter volumes of the above catalogue; and he is admitted to be the greatest dramatic genius the world has ever seen.

Now the writers of the Bible were for the most part men of very imperfect education, belonging to an insignificant people, dwelling in a little strip of land no larger than Wales, in a corner of Asia, where they were cut off from intercourse with the great literary nations of antiquity. If there were no Divine power guiding their intellect and furthering their work, how is it possible that it should have had such results? I would advise you to ponder carefully these facts on which I have been dwelling, to lay them up in your memory, and if a sceptic asks you (as the manner of sceptics is) to account for this or that particular statement or incident in the Bible on the supposition of its Divine origin, to show him that *he* has something far more difficult to account for if he denies its Divine origin. Tell him there may very probably be things here and there in Divine revelation which you cannot explain, but that he must meet you on the broad ground of what the Bible is and what it has done as a whole; and that before you enter into these details he must explain to you how it is that this Book, written by a number of obscure and apparently illiterate men, and, according to *his* statement, full of errors, contradictions, and absurdities, has survived all the attempts of kings and emperors to destroy it, all the efforts of learned men of many ages to refute it, and, in spite of all this, has achieved a success which the most brilliant writers of ancient or modern times have never attained, and has this day an influence on the thought and action of mankind to which no other book makes the faintest approach. He will find that very hard to explain. It *cannot* be explained except by admitting the truth, viz. that behind and through the intellect of the human authors of Scripture, the Spirit of God Himself was working, and that His hand has guided its history.

5. This, and only this, will explain another fact which the sceptic may be unwilling to admit, but which the impartial inquirer cannot gainsay,—that wherever this Book has been heartily received, diligently studied, and faithfully obeyed, there men have grown in virtue and godliness, there the principles of liberty have been developed, and the cause of humanity has prospered. The teachings of this Book have made the unchaste man pure, the drunkard sober, the

violent man gentle, and the selfish generous. They have sustained men under every kind of hardship, trial, and persecution; diffused rays of light through lives that would have been, without them, all gloom and sadness; and have enabled countless thousands to face the "Last Enemy" with calm cheerfulness, and even with ecstatic joy. Can the same be said of any other book in the whole realm of literature?

I have been the more anxious, dear friends, to set before you these considerations affecting the character and worth of the Book as a whole, because in the following chapters, in the study of the separate parts of the Bible, you may overlook the *unity* which belongs to it, and because in dwelling upon the human elements which it contains you may possibly lose sight of the Divine.

To some of you much of the ground traversed in this work will be wholly new. You have been accustomed to take the Bible as though it were a sacred volume, made by the Divine hand, which had dropped down to you out of heaven. It may be new, and perhaps at first even a little embarrassing, to learn that it *grew* gradually, during a period of above a thousand years; and to enter into discussions as to when and by whom particular books were written, and what special circumstances called them forth. But if you would teach this Book aright you must become acquainted with these things; and if your spirit is reverent, you will be willing to abandon any preconceived notions, and to ask simply, How has God been pleased to reveal His will? Now, it was not His pleasure to send us this Book miraculously, ready-made, complete. God's way was to enlighten men by His Holy Spirit by degrees, as they were able to bear it; each inspired man handing on to his successors what he had written, for their instruction and guidance, while they in turn looked up to God for fresh light, to disclose yet higher and deeper truths. You will find some further description of the Progress of Divine Revelation in the fourth chapter of this work. Every step of this process has the highest interest for us, and is fraught with instruction. The Bible cannot be rightly understood unless it is studied, as it was given, by degrees, step by step, "line upon line and precept upon precept." I trust you will not grudge the labour necessary to this thorough study. Remember that you have undertaken to teach and train a portion of the rising race in the most important of all kinds of knowledge. Remember that you have undertaken to expound to them the most wonderful book in all history, a book whose truly Divine origin and character has been above briefly indicated. In view of these considerations I trust you will brace up your energies to a diligent perusal of the following pages, fully resolved that whatever information they can give about this wonderful Book you will make that information your own. It will be of no use whatever to give this little work a slight reading. It must be thoroughly *studied*. The first two chapters in particular will require patient and earnest attention. Do not be discouraged if you cannot grasp the exact bearing of every point at the first perusal. There is nothing beyond your powers of comprehension if you will give your mind to the task, and you may have the consolation of knowing that you will find " plainer sailing " further on. Do not shirk the trouble of looking up the Scripture references. To have quoted the words at length would have increased this volume to nearly double its size ; but if you neglect to turn them up, you will miss a good deal of the profit you would otherwise gain, and in some cases miss the entire force of the argument. The Bible has come down to you in its present form through the almost infinite pain and labour of your forefathers. Surely it is not too much to expect that the heritage which they have won for you with sweat of brain and shedding of blood, will be by you at least diligently explored.

My little book makes no pretensions to originality. Most of what it contains, you will find said, and better said, elsewhere,—only, in books of larger cost, and less easily accessible to you. To some of those works I have referred you at the end of each chapter. Most of them will be found in any good library, and if you have access to such, you may study them there. The less expensive ones I hope you will by degrees make your own, and thus acquire for yourselves a Sunday school teacher's library, which will be of great assistance to you in your work. If the following pages arouse in your minds earnest desire to pursue Biblical study much further than they themselves can carry you, they will not have been written in vain. May the God who inspired "the Sunday School Text-book" aid you in all your endeavours to get at the "wealth of wisdom and knowledge hidden therein," and make this little book a useful instrument in your hand, as you seek to explore the mine, and bring forth its treasures for the enrichment of your classes.

Your affectionate Friend,

THE AUTHOR.

THE BIBLE:
THE SUNDAY SCHOOL TEXT-BOOK.

CHAPTER I.

ON THE EVIDENCES OF THE AUTHENTICITY AND GENUINENESS OF THE SACRED WRITINGS.

"We have not followed cunningly devised fables," says Peter, "when we made known unto you the power and coming of our Lord Jesus Christ;" and when the Sunday school teacher takes the Bible as his text-book, he should have a firm and rational conviction that he is not asking his class to follow cunningly devised fables, but a reliable record of the most momentous facts in the world's history. The sacred writings which constitute the record are divided into two portions, the Old and the New Testaments. In order of time the Old precedes the New; but for that very reason we shall first consider the evidences for the authenticity and genuineness of the writings which compose the New. They are nearer to us. The evidence is more accessible. If it is insufficient—if the writings of the New Testament are untrustworthy, it will be vain to prosecute our inquiry with reference to the still earlier writings of the Old; but on the other hand, if we can show that these books are genuine productions of the apostolic age, then we may use with confidence any evidence which they supply to establish the authority of the older scriptures.

1. New Testament.

St. Augustine, who wrote in the latter part of the fourth century, says, "We know the writings of the apostles as we know the works of Plato, Aristotle, Cicero, Varro, and others to be theirs, forasmuch as they have the testimony of contemporaries, and of those who lived in succeeding times. Shall any be so foolish and unreasonable as to deny or to dispute the credibility of such a testimony to the Scriptures which would be allowed in behalf of any writings whatever?"

This is true; but it is only part of the truth; for the testimony of succeeding authors to the authenticity of the apostolic writings is far stronger than any that can be adduced for the works of classical antiquity;* and Augustine leaves out of account the *internal evidence* derived from the writings themselves, which in many cases is of itself sufficient to show that they are genuine. We shall begin with this branch of evidence, and devote the most attention to it; because every reader can test it for himself. He does not need to take on trust a number of quotations from books that he has never seen; and to accept dates for their authorship which he has no means of verifying. He can take the New Testament by itself, and by careful examination of its contents satisfy himself that he is not "following cunningly devised fables;" that these writings are not the inventions of a later age, which the writers tried to pass off as the works of the apostles, but genuine productions of the apostolic men who laid the foundations of the Christian Church.

* See Appendix A.

1. *Internal Evidence (Pauline Epistles).*

When we examine the contents of the New Testament, we find first five books in the form of narrative; then a collection of letters, and last a writing of prophetic character. The first five books do not name their respective authors, the superscription ("Gospel according to Matthew," "Gospel according to Mark," etc.) being no part of the original document; but the first thirteen letters all purport to have been written by a person named Paul, who calls himself an apostle of Jesus Christ, and who is the central figure in the narrative treatise immediately preceding, *i.e.* the Book of Acts.

Let us begin with these letters that distinctly claim to be Paul's, and see whether the claim can be made good from internal evidence.

As to **General Characteristics**, we find first of all that they were certainly written by a Jew. Though the language is Greek, it contains Hebrew words and idioms. The quotations from the Old Testament are very numerous; they are generally introduced by the words "it is written," the common formula of the Jews in quoting their Scriptures. They contain many allusions to Jewish feasts and customs. The style of argument in some passages is just that which we know was employed by Jewish Rabbis; the dignity and special prerogatives of the Jewish nation are maintained; and the eloquent outburst of feeling in Rom. ix. 1-5 could only have proceeded from a devout and enthusiastic Jew. The writer himself tells us that he was brought up after the strictest sect of the Jewish religion; and the whole style of the letters is in keeping with that statement. We next observe that the writer had evidently been a bitter persecutor of Christianity at first, but was after his conversion imbued with the spirit of the gospel in its deepest, broadest, freest form; rising completely above the narrowness and sectarianism of his Jewish training, denouncing all attempts to impose Jewish rites on the converts from heathenism, addressing himself for the most part to Gentiles, and as "the apostle of the Gentiles" "magnifying his office." We observe further, that though the writer must have been a Jew by birth and training, he had evidently been brought into closest contact with Greek civilization. The language he writes is good Greek, with the slight Hebrew colouring noted above. He frequently draws illustrations from the Greek games. He quotes from a Greek poet in 1 Cor. xv. 33, and from another in Titus i. 12. All these features in the Epistles harmonize exactly with what we are told of Paul in the Book of Acts—that he was a Jew; born at Tarsus, a Greek colony; brought up at the feet of Gamaliel, the great Jewish rabbi; a vehement persecutor of the Church until his conversion, and then commissioned by Christ to be especially the apostle to the Gentiles. Many incidents of his life reported in the Acts are incidentally alluded to in the Epistles, and both agree in representing him to have been specially hated and persecuted by the Jews, and even encountering some suspicion and opposition from his Jewish fellow Christians on account of the broad free gospel which he preached to the Gentiles, and his indifference to the punctilios of Jewish ritual. Moreover, the Epistles are full of allusions to persons and places mentioned in the Book of Acts, and which harmonize exactly with what we read of them there. Now, it is hardly possible that any individual in a later age, trying to write as Paul would have written, should have succeeded in securing perfect agreement in all these manifold ways through this long series of letters. He would have been almost certain to fall into contradictions of some kind, either in small matters of fact or in points of style, language, mode of thought, and doctrinal bearing.

On these general grounds we should conclude that they

are by that Paul whose name they bear, and who is mentioned in the Book of Acts.

But further, this conclusion is rendered absolutely certain by the **undesigned coincidences** which may be discovered in these letters. Even if it were thought possible that, by using very great care, some designing person might have contrived to preserve the agreement as far as we have yet traced it; we shall find, on still closer examination, points of agreement so *minute*, so *casual*, so evidently *unintentional*, that no forger could possibly have thought of inventing them. We will give a few instances from the *first four* Epistles.

We take up the **Epistle to the Romans**, and we read (xv. 25, 26), "Now I go unto Jerusalem to minister unto the saints. For it hath pleased them of Macedonia and Achaia to make a certain contribution for the poor saints which are at Jerusalem." Here Paul speaks of a collection that had been made in two European Churches for the poor brethren in Jerusalem, the proceeds of which were to be taken thither by Paul himself. Now, turning to 2 Cor. viii. 1–4, we read, "Moreover, brethren, we do you to wit of the grace of God bestowed on the Churches of Macedonia, how that in a great trial of affliction the abundance of their joy and of their deep poverty abounded unto the riches of their liberality. For to their power, I bear record, yea, and beyond their power they were willing of themselves; praying us with much entreaty that we would receive the gift, and take upon us the fellowship of the ministering to the saints." See also ix. 1, 2: "I know the forwardness of your mind . . . that Achaia was ready a year ago." Neither of these passages say *what* poor saints the collection was for; but if we now turn to 1 Cor. xvi. 1–4 (remembering that Corinth was the capital of Achaia) we there find Paul giving directions about this same collection, and adding, "When I come, whomsoever ye shall approve by your letters, them will I send to bring your liberality unto *Jerusalem*. And if it be meet that I go also, they shall go with me." Here we have the *place* mentioned to which the contributions were destined, but these passages still leave it uncertain whether Paul did actually bring these contributions to Jerusalem, as stated in the Epistle to the Romans. So we take up the Book of Acts. There we read first of his purpose to travel through Macedonia and Achaia (the very places where the collections were to be made) to Jerusalem (xix. 21). Then we find (xx. and xxi.), that he executed his purpose and duly reached Jerusalem; only nothing is said yet of any collection: but after he has been taken prisoner and carried to Cæsarea, when he is making his defence before the governor Felix, and arguing that he had done no harm to the Jews, it drops out quite incidentally that he had brought these contributions with him. "Now after many years (*i.e.* of absence from Jerusalem) I came to bring alms to my nation, and offerings" (Acts xxiv. 17).

So the statement with which we began in the Epistle to the Romans is confirmed in all its parts. But the confirmation has to be hunted up from three different writings and half a dozen different passages. It is evidently *not the work of design*. It would never have occurred to a forger of the Epistles to put in those three scattered passages in the Corinthians merely to establish something that he had said quite incidentally in the Epistle to the Romans. Still less could the writer of the Book of Acts have been thinking about these texts in the Epistles, and put in that piece in Paul's defence before Felix for the sake of confirming them. All these allusions come in quite naturally in their own place. They are evidently undesigned, but they fit in exactly. They could only occur so in the writings of one actually concerned in the events. Hence they not only prove the genuineness of the Epistles, but show that the *Book of Acts* is authentic history. Many other similar cases of undesigned coincidences might be cited from the Romans.

Take up now the **First Epistle to the Corinthians**. The whole of the circumstances under which the Epistle was written, and the way they came out, though perfectly natural in themselves, are not such as it would have been at all likely that a forger should invent. It appears from 1 Cor. vii. 1, that the Corinthians had written a letter to Paul asking for direction upon certain matters of interest to the Church, such as the desirability of marriage, the lawfulness of eating things that had been offered to idols, etc. It also appears, from other parts of the Epistle, that there were certain disgraceful proceedings in the Church at Corinth, about which the Corinthians had not said a word in their letter, but of which Paul had heard through other sources. "It hath been declared unto me of you, my brethren, *by them which are of the house of Chloe*, that there are contentions among you" (i. 11). Again, "It is *reported* commonly that there is fornication among you" (v. 1). Again, "When ye come together . . . *I hear* that there be divisions among you; and I partly believe it" (xi. 18). Paul is so distressed at this, that he occupies six chapters of the Epistle in reproving them for these faults, and not till the seventh chapter does he take up the questions on which they had written to him. Not till then, and then almost incidentally, does he mention their letter at all "Now concerning the things whereof ye wrote unto me," etc. (vii. 1). Now, how natural all this is on the supposition that the letter is genuine; how natural that the Corinthians should have said nothing in their letter about the scandals in their Church, and that the bad news should only have come to Paul in a roundabout way. But these very grave scandals having come to his knowledge, how natural that they should be the first thing he takes notice of. How extremely *improbable* that any *forger* should go to work in this fashion, first conceiving the idea of Paul's writing a letter to the Corinthians in answer to one received from them, and yet suppressing all mention of their letter till he was half-way through the Epistle. On the face of it the Epistle is genuine. Let us, however, examine some of the particular coincidences. In 1 Cor. iv. 12, Paul says, describing his toilsome life, "We labour working with our hands;" as likewise in 1 Thess. ii. 9, "Ye remember, brethren, our labour and travail: for labouring night and day because we would not be chargeable unto any of you, we preached unto you the gospel of God." Now turn to Acts xviii. 1-3, and you find these statements confirmed. Paul came to Corinth, and finding a certain Jew, Apollos, with his wife Priscilla, "because he was the same craft, he abode with them, *and wrought*: for by their occupation they were tentmakers."

For another coincidence in this epistle turn to i. 12, "Every one of you saith, I am of Paul; and I of Apollos; and I of Cephas," etc. Also to iii. 4-6, "One saith, I am of Paul; and another, I am of Apollos. . . . Who then is Paul, and who is Apollos, but ministers by whom ye believed? . . . *I have planted, Apollos watered;* but God gave the increase." Now, when we examine the Book of Acts, we find that this is just what is represented as actually taking place. Paul *founded* the Church, and Apollos *strengthened* it. In Acts xviii. 1, we read that Paul departed from Athens and came to Corinth. There he preached the gospel, and (ver. 8) "many of the Corinthians believed, and were baptized." He then left Corinth and went into Asia, continuing there a long time (vv. 18-23). Now, in the remainder of this eighteenth chapter (vv. 24-28) we read that *Apollos* passed from Ephesus to Achaia, and "when he was come, *helped them much which had believed through grace.*" Corinth was the capital of Achaia, and there Apollos fixed his headquarters, as we learn from xix. 1. The agreement is clear, yet no one can imagine that this history is invented to support the passage in Paul's Epistle; or that this allusion in the Epistle was introduced for the sake of accordance with the Book of Acts. It is only the figure which Paul employs, "planting and watering," from which the reader *infers* that it was he who came first to Corinth and founded the Church, and Apollos came afterwards and strengthened it; and is hence enabled to trace its agreement with the Book of Acts. A forger, if he had used the figure at all, would very likely have said, "Apollos planted and Paul watered," and thus have been betrayed into error. And if the agreement had been artificial and designed, the third name, Cephas (Peter), in connection with the Corinthian Church would either have been introduced into the history or omitted from the Epistle.

The **Second Epistle to the Corinthians** is written chiefly to congratulate the Church on the effect which the First Epistle had produced on them. Paul had rebuked them sharply for their faults, and being anxious to learn how they received his admonition before he saw them again, he arranged that Titus should start from Corinth and bring him word, meeting him somewhere on his way from Ephesus to Corinth. For his report he waited most anxiously. Now read carefully 2 Cor. ii. 1-13 and vii. 2-16, and ask yourself whether these touching passages, in which we seem to see the very throbbing of the apostle's heart, could possibly be the fictitious utterances of some cool designer endeavouring to pass off his work as Paul's. One example of coincidence between this Epistle and the history we have already noticed in dealing with the Romans. We find another in 2 Cor. xi. 9, as compared with Acts xviii. 1, 5. In the first passage we read, "When I was present with you" (*i.e.* present in Corinth), "and wanted, I was chargeable to no man: for that which was lacking to me the *brethren which came from Macedonia* supplied." In the Acts we read, "After these things, Paul departed from Athens and came to Corinth. . . . And when Silas and Timotheus were come from Macedonia, Paul was pressed in the spirit, and testified to the Jews that Jesus was

Christ." Here the arrival of the brethren is mentioned, at the time specified in the Epistle, viz. on the occasion of Paul's first visit to Corinth. But the coincidence is not *contrived*, for this visit of the brethren is mentioned in the Epistle quite incidentally, in the endeavour to show the Corinthians that, though he had received gifts from other Churches, he neither received nor desired any gift from them. Another plain coincidence is found on comparing 2 Cor. xi. 32, 33 with Acts ix. 23–25. This agreement is indeed, so obvious, that it might be looked on as the result of design, were it not certain upon other grounds that the writer of the Acts was not borrowing from the Epistle, nor the writer of the Epistle from the Acts. We cannot here state all these grounds; let one suffice. We have just seen that the writer of the Acts speaks of *Silas* and Timotheus being with Paul at Corinth. In 2 Cor. i. 19 we read, " Jesus Christ, who was preached among you by us, even by me and *Silvanus* and Timotheus, was not yea and nay." Now we are quite justified in regarding Silas as a shortened form of Silvanus (like Austin for Augustine); but, assuredly, if the authors of the Acts and the Epistle had borrowed from one another, they would have kept exactly the same name in both books. Note, in passing, that we have in the presence of these two brethren another coincidence between the letters and the history.

The **Epistle to the Galatians** presents numerous points of agreement with the account of Paul's life given in the Acts. Compare Gal. i. 13, 14 with Acts vii. 58, viii. 1, 3, xxii. 3–5, and xxvi. 4, 5; also Gal. i. 17, 18 (which implies a long residence at Damascus) with Acts ix. 22, 23; also Gal. i. 22–24 (where " the Churches in Judæa " evidently means the Churches outside Jerusalem) with Acts ix. 26–28; and Gal. ii. 1 with Acts xv. 2. Notice, further, the fact that as in the Epistle Paul constantly speaks of himself as opposed to the *Jews*, " them that were under the law," " them of the circumcision," and as suffering persecution from them (Gal. ii. 11–14; iv. 29; v. 4, 11; vi. 12); so in the Book of Acts it is nearly always the *Jews* who either assault Paul themselves, or stir up the heathen to persecute him. See Acts xiii. 49, 50; xiv. 1, 2, 19; xvii. 4, 5. In Gal. iv. 13, 14, we have an allusion to an infirmity, or temptation in the flesh, which is, no doubt, the same as "the thorn in the flesh" (2 Cor. xii. 7–9); but the language in which it is referred to is so different, and the reason for referring to it so different, that it is impossible to think the one was *designed* in imitation or corroboration of the other.

One other mark of genuineness in this Epistle should be noted. The main doctrine of the Epistle to the Galatians is the same as that of the Epistle to the Romans, viz. that a man is justified by faith without the works of the law. But, while this doctrine is supported in Romans purely by argument, it is backed up in Galatians by assertion of the personal authority of the writer, and appeal to the affection which the readers had shown for him in time past. See Gal. iii. 1; iv. 11, 14–16; v. 2, 10. Now, if these are the genuine letters of Paul, and if the account of his labours in the Acts is authentic, this difference is quite natural and intelligible. We have seen that the Epistle to the Romans was written when Paul was setting out for that journey to Jerusalem mentioned in Acts xx., and at that time *he had not yet been in Rome*, as appears likewise from Rom. i. 13. Hence he could not appeal to his Roman readers on the score of their personal love and reverence for him. He could only reason with them on scriptural and general grounds. But, if the Acts be true, he had himself planted these Churches in Galatia, and watched over them with pastoral fidelity. Hence, in the Epistle to the Galatians, those appeals to their affection and veneration for his person are quite appropriate. But a person sitting down to forge these letters in the name of Paul would never have thought of making this nice distinction in the style of argument.

Now these are only fragmentary *specimens* of the abundant internal evidence of the genuineness of these documents. The attentive student will discover many others. On this ground alone we should feel justified in saying that these four Epistles (Romans, 1 Corinthians, 2 Corinthians, and Galatians) are certainly the work of the apostle Paul who is mentioned in the Book of Acts. But to "make assurance doubly sure," and at the same time to illustrate a branch of evidence of great importance in establishing the authenticity of other books of the New Testament, let us see what testimony we have to their Pauline authorship from *external* sources.

2. *External Testimony (Pauline Epistles).*

We preface our inquiry by this remark, that since we have seen that these four Epistles, by whomsoever written, are indisputably *all from the same hand*, testimony to the Pauline authorship of any one of them is virtually testimony to the Pauline authorship of all four. Now, there has come down to us a letter written by a certain man named **Clement** (possibly the Clement alluded to in Phil. iv. 3), who was an elder in the Church at Rome towards the end of the first century, who therefore must certainly have been born before Paul died. This letter is addressed to the Church at Corinth, and it contains these words, "Take up the Epistle of the blessed Paul. What did he first write to you in the beginning of the gospel? Of a truth he wrote to you of the Spirit concerning *himself* and *Cephas* and *Apollos, because ye had even then formed parties.*" No one can doubt that he refers to what Paul wrote in 1 Cor. i. 11, 12, and the rest of Clement's letter contains numerous quotations from this same Epistle. It also contains these words, "Casting off from us all unrighteousness and iniquity and covetousness, debates, malignities and deceits, whisperings and backbitings, pride and boasting, vainglory and inhospitality, for they that do such things are hateful to God, and not only they that do them, but those that have pleasure in the same." Now it is true that Clement does not here say that he is quoting Paul; nor is this an *exact* quotation of Rom. i. 29–32; but if you will turn to that passage you will feel convinced that Clement must have seen it, and had it in his mind when he wrote the foregoing sentence. He was an elder of the Church at Rome, and his words afford clear testimony that our Epistle to the Romans was written to and received by that Church.

With this unmistakable evidence, dating from the apostolic age itself, it is almost superfluous to adduce further and later testimony, and we shall forbear quoting the passages in full. **Polycarp**, Bishop of Smyrna, who was a disciple of the apostle John, wrote a letter to the Philippians which has been preserved; and in it we find quotations from Romans, 1 Corinthians, and Galatians, with a probable reference to 2 Corinthians. **Marcion** and **Basilides**, the founders of two heretical sects, who lived about the same time (A.D. 120–130), made use of all the four Epistles we have been studying. They do not mention Paul by name as the author, but when, as heretics, they appeal to these Epistles in defence of their position, it shows that the Epistles were then accepted as of apostolic authority. Three other writers, **Valentinus**, **Heracleon**, and **Ptolemæus**, who flourished about A.D. 150, also refer to these Epistles. In the second half of that century we find these Epistles in general use among the Churches both of the East and West, and constantly quoted as Paul's, *e.g.* by **Theophilus** of Antioch, **Irenæus**, **Clement** of Alexandria, **Tertullian**, and, in fact, by all the Church Fathers whose works have come down to us. If any further testimony were needed, we might point to two ancient translations of the Scriptures, the **Syriac** and the **Old Latin**, which were certainly made before the end of the second century. Had any one of these Epistles been spurious or of doubtful authority, it certainly would not have been included in these translations; but there we find them all.

We have selected these Epistles as our starting point. We see that their genuineness and authenticity are proved beyond all possibility of doubt. The internal evidence alone would have been sufficient; but it is further supported by external testimony much stronger than can be adduced in support of any work of classical antiquity, such as the histories of Livy and Tacitus or the poems of Horace and Virgil.

We have not space to give the evidence for the other books of the New Testament with the same fulness of detail. It is the same in *kind*, both internal and external, though, for reasons which want of space forbids our stating, not always so full in measure. In the chapter on the Canon the student will find a table from which the strength of the external testimony to any particular book of the New Testament can be measured at a glance. Our object has been to show clearly the *method* by which the genuineness and authenticity of the New Testament Scriptures are established, and we will now point out how the certain authenticity of these four Epistles affords a sure basis for demonstrating the authenticity of the other books.

3. *The Gospels and other Books of the New Testament.*

We have already seen how in proving the authenticity of Romans, Corinthians, and Galatians the veracity of the Book of Acts is established at the same time by the method of undesigned coincidences. These four Epistles further supply us with a test by which we can try the other Epistles ascribed to Paul. We now know for certain his style of writing, his mode of argument, his favourite illustrations, his pet words and phrases. When we find these same recurring in the Epistles to the Ephesians, Philippians, Colossians, etc., it is so much confirmatory proof (in addition to a mass of testimony similar to that we have investigated in the case of the first four) that they are from his pen. In this way, where the other evidence is not so strong as that for the first four, the deficiency is supplied by comparison with them, and the marks of identity of authorship thus discovered.

But still further, these Epistles have a very important bearing on the authenticity of the Gospels. They do not, indeed, quote the Gospels, for the very simple reason that the Gospels were not then written; but they incidentally refer to the main facts of Christ's history. We have in these four letters—written, be it remembered, within a few years of the crucifixion, by a man who lived in Jerusalem itself, and held office under the very Council that put Christ to death—testimony to the following facts: That Christ traced His descent from David (Rom. i. 3); that He was born of a human mother, but was in His spiritual nature the Son of God (Gal. iv. 4; Rom. i. 4); that He had human brothers (1 Cor. ix. 5); that He led a life of self-denial, humiliation, poverty, and persecution (Rom. xv. 3; 2 Cor. viii. 9); that He lived in general conformity with the laws of Moses (Rom. xv. 8); that He had disciples whom He named apostles, and that their number was twelve (Gal. i. 17; 1 Cor. xv. 5, 7); that he endowed them with the power of working miracles (compare 2 Cor. xii. 12 with Luke ix. 1, 2 and Mark xvi. 14–18); that among these apostles James, Cephas, and John enjoyed a kind of pre-eminence (Gal. ii. 9); that Cephas was also called Peter, and that he was a married man (compare Gal. ii. 8–10, 1 Cor. ix. 5 with Mark i. 30); that Christ, was betrayed, and that (the same night) He instituted the Lord's Supper with the words which we find recorded in the evangelists (1 Cor. xi. 23–25); that He was crucified, and that His death was a ransom for many (Rom. v. 6–8;

Gal. ii. 20, and many other passages); that He was buried, rose again on the third day, and was seen by the apostles and many other disciples who were living at the time when Paul wrote (1 Cor. xv. 4-6); that He finally ascended into heaven to the right hand of God (Rom. viii. 34), and was believed by the early Church to rule with all power in heaven and earth according to His word in the Gospels (1 Cor. xv. 25).*

We have here the main facts of the gospel history certified by a contemporary living on the spot within thirty years of the crucifixion. Of course this does not of itself prove the genuineness of the Gospels; but it does prove that the representation of Christ which they give was the representation received by the Church from the very first. It shows that if the opponents of Christianity could destroy the credit of the Gospels (which they cannot), there would still remain indisputable evidence of the supernatural events on which Christianity rests; for the evidence is supplied by these four letters, the genuineness of which is admitted by these opponents themselves. It also goes far to establish the veracity of the Gospels in all respects, for if a witness is proved to be correct in some of his statements by another independent witness, it is always assumed, in the absence of any distinct evidence

---

* The reader will note the above facts are cited from the first four Epistles only. If we take the other Epistles we find reference to the following additional events in our Lord's life. The temptation (Heb. ii. 18, iv. 15); the transfiguration (2 Pet. ii. 17, 18); the agony in the garden (Heb. v. 7); the trial before Pontius Pilate (1 Tim. vi. 13); and the fact that the place where he was crucified was outside Jerusalem (Heb. xiii. 12). It may also be inferred from the Pauline Epistles that Christ had instituted the ordinance of baptism (Rom. vi. 3; Gal. iii. 27; 1 Cor. i. 13-17). It may seem odd to quote the words, "Christ sent me not to baptize, but to preach the gospel," as a proof that Christ instituted baptism; but the meaning undoubtedly is, "Christ sent me indeed to baptize; but *much more* to preach the gospel." It is well the Sunday school teacher should bear in mind that this is almost always the force of this construction ("not," etc., "but," etc.). Let him refer for confirmation to Matt. x. 20; John vii. 16, xii. 44, xiv. 24.

to the contrary, that his other statements are correct also.

But this is far from being the only evidence in favour of the Gospels.

The internal evidence and the external testimony are little inferior to that for the Pauline Epistles. As in these last, so in the four evangelists, there are innumerable coincidences which cannot be the result of design: for, though they agree in all important points, there are a number of small differences and apparent contradictions which show that no one of the Gospels could have been copied from the others. Such differences almost always occur in the testimony of any witnesses, however truthful, who give their testimony independently of each other. A complete knowledge of all the circumstances would no doubt enable us to reconcile most of the discrepancies, as we shall show later on in the section "Scripture Difficulties." As it is, they are of value, as showing that the four accounts are independent. Their authentic character is further confirmed by comparison of their contents with other than Scripture writers. They contain many allusions to persons, places, and events in Palestine, which have been verified from other sources of information. The simplicity of the narratives, the graphic touches here and there, and the minute details given concerning many of the events point to eye-witnesses or those who had received information from eye-witnesses, as the authors. They are not at all like the inventions of fiction in a crude and unliterary age. Moreover, as in the case of the Epistles, so in the case of the Gospels, a series of writers from the beginning of the second century onwards quote them, and refer to them as of Divine authority. A few specimens of this evidence must suffice.

Papias was a companion of Polycarp, who was a disciple of the apostle John. He professes to have gathered his information from those who had seen Jesus and from their followers. And he says he heard from them that "Matthew wrote his oracles in Hebrew, and every one interpreted them as best he could;" and that "Mark, having become the interpreter of Peter, wrote down accurately whatever he remembered of what was either said or done by Christ."

Justin, a native of Samaria, addressed an Apology or Defence of Christianity to the Roman emperor between the years 140 and 150 A.D., which has been preserved. In it he says, speaking of the Lord's Supper, that "the apostles in the memoirs composed by them, which are called Gospels, have thus delivered it, that Jesus commanded them to take bread and give thanks," etc. Again: "In the commentaries, which, as I have said, were composed by the apostles and their followers, it is written that His sweat fell like drops of blood." Justin also tells us that "the memoirs of the apostles or the writings of the prophets were read when the Christians assembled for worship," showing that they were treated with the same veneration as the Old Testament Scriptures.

Irenæus, who became Bishop of Lyons in A.D. 177, tells us that "Matthew among the Jews wrote a Gospel in their own language. . . . Mark also, the disciple and interpreter of Peter, delivered to us in writing the things that had been preached by Peter; and Luke, the companion of Paul, put down in a book the gospel that had been preached by him. Afterwards John, the disciple of the Lord, who also leaned on His breast, likewise put forth a Gospel while he dwelt at Ephesus in Asia."

We have passed over many slight references to one or other of the Gospels in writers who lived between Papias and Irenæus. And after the latter date they were so universally used and acknowledged as apostolic that it would be absurd to attempt to quote the testimony. If it seems strange to the reader, that if the Gospels were really written by the apostles and their immediate followers, it should be so long before they all came into general use, and that they are not more frequently quoted by writers in the early part of the second century, he must remember, first, that printing was not then invented; every copy had to be made by hand, and consequently they multiplied very slowly: and, secondly, that the facilities for communication between one place and another were not nearly so great as they are now; and the Churches were not then organized into one body; so that one of them might possess and use a Gospel for many years which another Church in a distant province had never seen. If, as some would have us believe, they were not written till the middle of the second century, it would have been quite impossible that before the end of that century we should find them, as we do, spread over all the Churches of Europe, Asia, and Africa, and everywhere acknowledged to be of Divine authority.

One other evidence in favour of the genuineness and authenticity of our Gospels may be noticed. Sceptical writers say these Gospels were made up hundreds of years after the time of Christ, out of vague traditions, floating myths, and the imagination of the writers. Now, we really have some such works as these—the so-called "Gospel of Thomas," the "Gospel of Nicodemus," etc. We recommend the Sunday school teacher to look into them if he has the opportunity. When he has scanned the silly stories, the absurd miracles, the palpable exaggerations, the incongruities of character, and contradictions of fact, which they contain,—to say nothing of the pretentious style in which they are written, and the prurient curiosity which they attempt to gratify,—he will turn to the sublimely pure and simple narrative of the four evangelists with a firmer conviction than ever of its genuine character and inspired worth. He will see what sort of a life of Christ we should have had if it had been written as the sceptics would have us believe, and how vast the difference between such mythical products of a later age and the authentic history of the New Testament.

II. Old Testament.

The strongest evidence we have for the trustworthiness and Divine authority of the books of the Old Testament is the way in which they are employed by the writers of the New, and by Christ Himself. Many circumstances conspire to prevent our having the same evidence for the genuineness and authenticity of the separate books, that we have for the Gospels and Epistles of the New Testament, such as the extreme antiquity of the books themselves, the long period over which the writing of them extended, the fact that this was not an active literary period, so that there is hardly any contemporary Jewish literature outside the Canon which might be referred to in confirmation of its contents, and the entire isolation of the Jews from other nations in respect of their religion. No doubt the same methods which we have followed in the case of the New might be *partially* applied to the Old. In the Psalms and the Prophets there are many allusions which confirm the authority of the historical books according to the method of undesigned coincidences. The contents of those books may also be in a measure verified by evidence drawn from external sources. Thus, the ancient traditions of all Eastern countries and many Western tell of a great deluge in the early history of man, and the escape of a favoured family by means of a floating vessel. The monuments of Egypt exhibit the slavery of the Hebrews under the Pharaohs. The Assyrian tablets record the wars of Sennacherib and his successors against the Jews, and mention by name many of the Jewish kings. On the Arch of Titus, still standing at Rome, erected to commemorate his capture of Jerusalem, there is a representation of a seven-branched candlestick borne as a trophy, which is in all probability a copy of the one taken from the Jewish temple. The Septuagint, a Greek version of the Hebrew Scriptures, made in the third century B.C., contains all the books of our Old Testament. We have, further, a history of the Jews, written by Josephus in the first century of our era, which agrees in all important particulars with the history as given in our Old Testament Scriptures. And he also cites most of the Old Testament books by name. But far beyond the value of these testimonies to the veracity of the Sacred Writings, is the simple fact that Christ and His apostles used them as books of Divine authority, quoted their statements with unwavering confidence, and their prophecies as words that must be fulfilled.

The following Old Testament books are quoted from, or their contents distinctly referred to *by Christ Himself*:—

Genesis	*See* Matt. xix. 4, 5.
Exodus	,, Matt. xv. 4; Luke xx. 37.
Leviticus	,, Matt. xxii. 39.
Deuteronomy	,, Matt. iv. 4, 7, 10.
1 Samuel	,, Mark ii. 26.
1 Kings	,, Luke iv. 25, 26, and xi. 31.
2 Kings	,, Luke iv. 27.
2 Chronicles	,, Matt. xxiii. 35.
Psalms	,, Luke xx. 42, and many other passages.
Proverbs	,, Luke xiv. 8–10.
Isaiah	,, Luke iv. 17-19, and many other passages.
Jeremiah	,, Matt. xxi. 13.
Daniel	,, Mark xiii. 14.
Hosea	,, Matt. xii. 7.
Jonah	,, Luke xi. 30–32.
Micah	,, Matt. x. 35.
Zechariah	,, Matt. xxi. 4, 5.
Malachi	,, Matt. xi. 10.

In the writings of the evangelists and apostles, besides many other references to the books already cited by Jesus Christ Himself, the following are referred to:—*

---

* It will be understood that we have merely given *one* reference to each Old Testament book as a specimen. It has been computed that there are altogether 265 direct quotations from the Old Testament in the New, besides 350 obvious allusions. See Augus's "Bible Handbook," p. 80.

Numbers	. . . . .	*See* 1 Cor. x. 6–9.
Joshua	. . . . . .	,, Heb. xi. 30-31.
Judges	. . . . . .	,, Heb. xi. 32.
Ruth	. . . .	,, Matt. i. 5.
Job	. . . .	,, James v. 11.
Ezekiel	. . . . . .	,, Rev. xxii. 2.
Haggai	. . . . . .	,, Heb. xii. 26.
Habakkuk	. . . . . .	,, Rom. i. 17.
Joel	. . . . . .	,, Acts ii. 16, 17.
Amos	. . . . .	,, Acts vii. 42, 43.

Hence we see that out of the thirty-nine books of the Old Testament we have quotations from, or distinct references to thirty,* either by Christ or by His apostles, and they are referred to as books having a Divine origin, and a recognized authority. Not only so, but the name of Moses is connected by Christ with the authorship of the Pentateuch, and the name of David with the Psalms.† That in many cases the Scriptures of the Old Testament are quoted without mentioning the author of the particular book need not surprise us; for it was not then so generally the practice, as it is now, to name the author in quoting a book; and even now, in quoting texts, it is frequently deemed sufficient to say, "the Bible says," or "we read in the Scriptures," without giving a more particular reference. So the common Jewish formula in quoting from the Old Testament was simply "It is written," or "The Scripture saith." It will further be shown, when we treat in the next chapter of the formation of the Canon, that prior to

---

* 1 and 2 Samuel formed originally one book; they were only divided for convenience in later times. Similarly 1 and 2 Kings and 1 and 2 Chronicles. Hence a reference to either portion is testimony to the whole.

† Christ does not assert that Moses wrote all the Pentateuch any more than he asserts that David wrote all the Psalms. It is quite certain that Moses did not record his own death (Deut. xxxiv.); and modern research has traced the hand of several authors in the Pentateuch, as well as in the Book of Psalms. But Christ's words at the least imply that the law of God, which forms the core and centre of the Pentateuch, was by the hand of Moses, just as the Psalms of David undoubtedly form the nucleus of that collection; and He gives to both books as a whole the sanction of His authority.

the time of Christ the books of the Old Testament had been collected, and, with one or two doubtful exceptions in the case of some of the smaller books, were certainly the same that we have in our Bibles now. They were divided into three parts, known as the Law, the Prophets, and the Sacred Writings, of which last division the Psalms formed the principal portion; and they are frequently referred to by Christ under this division, particularly in Luke xxiv. 44, where he says, "These are the words that I spoke unto you while I was yet with you that all things must be fulfilled that were written in the law of Moses, and in the Prophets, and in the Psalms concerning Me." From all this we may certainly conclude, that our Old Testament was Christ's Bible; and this fully compensates for the lack of evidence which would enable us to determine the human authorship of each several book with the same precision that is attainable in the case of the New Testament Scriptures.

We conclude this chapter with a quotation from the Rev. Dr. Stanley Leathes, which extends further the argument last employed, and may fitly sum up the whole. "The interdependence of the Old Testament and the New, at once undesigned and impossible as the result of connivance or collusion, separated as they are by an interval of 450 years, and both the combined result of various minds in various ages; the Old Testament containing as it does the germ and nucleus of the New, and the New containing the realization and fulfilment of the Old, not as a matter of contrivance, but as a matter of broad and patent history, is one of the most convincing proofs of their essential unity, the two parts corresponding like a cloven tally; and it must ever remain an irrefragable proof of the Divine origin of Christianity. At all events, the phenomenon is unique in the history and literature of the world"

BOOKS FOR REFERENCE AND FURTHER STUDY.

"Not of Man, but of God," by J. M. Manning, D.D. D. Lothrop & Co. $1.00.

Paley's "Horæ Paulinæ," with additional essays by Dean Howson. $1.10.

Stanley's "Jewish Church," vol. ii. Appendix on the Authorship of the Books of the Old Testament. Carters. 3 vols., $3.00 for the set.

Erskine's "Internal Evidence." Draper. 75 cts.

Sayce's "Fresh Light from the Ancient Monuments." London Religious Tract Society. $1.50.

Wright's "Divine Authority of the Bible." $1.25. "Logic of Christian Evidences." $1.50.

For advanced students, acquainted with the Greek and Latin languages.

"Our Gospels in the Second Century," by Dr. Sanday. Macmillan. $3.00.

"Introduction to the Study of the Gospels," by Canon Westcott. Macmillan. $3.00.

CHAPTER II.

ON THE FORMATION OF THE CANON—CHARACTERISTICS OF THE SEVERAL BOOKS.

THE word Canon is originally a Greek word meaning a straight rod, or carpenter's rule. Hence it came to signify a rule or standard of any kind for testing and judging things, whether of a material or spiritual nature. As applied to the books of Scripture the adjective "canonical" came into use before the substantive "canon." Those books which embodied God's rule of righteousness were called "canonical." When these were collected together, that collection was called the Canon. The word is generally used as distinguishing the books of Scripture from certain other books called uncanonical, or apocryphal. About the time when the latest books of the Old Testament were written, or shortly afterwards, appeared many other books containing Jewish history, pious narratives, and religious maxims, such as the Books of the Maccabees, the Book of Wisdom, etc., which though highly esteemed (and some of them of great historic value) were not deemed to come up to the standard of intrinsic worth and fulness of inspiration which entitled them to be regarded as of Divine authority. They were therefore excluded from the Canon of the Old Testament. Similarly in the post-apostolic age there were some writings, such as the Epistle of Clement and the Epistle of Barnabas, which, though undoubtedly written by good men, fell short of the authority which Christ had given to His apostles, and, though much read by the early Christians, were not placed on the same footing with the apostolic writings, but remained outside the Canon.

We have already traced the evidence for the genuineness and authenticity of some of the principal books, and exemplified the methods followed in the case of all. We would now indicate the stages by which the *collection* was formed, beginning with the Old Testament.

1. CANON OF THE OLD TESTAMENT.

First Division, "The Law."—We read in Deut. xxxi. 24–26, "It came to pass, when Moses had made an end of writing the words of this law in a book, until they were finished, that Moses commanded the Levites, which bare the ark of the covenant of the Lord, saying, 'Take this book of the law, and put it in the side" (not *inside*, but *beside;* see 1 Kings viii. 9) "of the Ark of the Covenant of the Lord your God, that it may be there for a witness.'" This book, no doubt, was substantially the same as the Pentateuch, or first five books of Scripture; though it received some further revisions and the additional account of the death of Moses himself. This, the germ of our Old Testament Canon, was for a long time the whole Canon, and was always regarded with peculiar reverence. It is constantly referred to as forming the first division of the Canon under the name of "the Law." We find distinct mention of this book in the reign of Josiah, when Hilkiah the high priest said unto Shaphan the scribe, "I have found the book of the law in the house of the Lord." It would appear to have been long neglected, and when it was read before the king, he was much distressed to find that its precepts had not been obeyed (2 Kings xxii. 8–13).

Second Division, "The Prophets."—The historical books which follow the Pentateuch were written at various intervals between the entrance to Canaan and the Captivity, but there is no evidence of any collection of them into a Canon till the time of Nehemiah. It was natural that at that time, when the nation was being re-established, and the worship of God re-organized, after the disorder and disruption of the exile, that the leaders of the people should gather together the records of God's dealings with their fathers, and what he had taught them in later days by the prophets, and lay them up for a memorial and Divine testimony. Accordingly, while Ezra and Nehemiah instructed the people afresh out of the old Canon, "the law" (Neh. viii.), they also compiled the second great division of the Old Testament Canon, as we read in the Second Book of Maccabees ii. 13, that Nehemiah gathered together "the Acts of the Kings and the Prophets, and the Psalms of David." The Psalms of David, with others added to them, were subsequently transferred to another section of the Canon. But the other books collected by Ezra and Nehemiah form a second well-marked division of the Jewish Canon, commonly called "the prophets." It included Joshua, Judges, First and Second of Samuel, First and Second of Kings, Isaiah, Jeremiah, and Ezekiel, and the twelve minor prophets, Hosea, Joel, Amos, etc., to Malachi. The application of the term "prophets" to the *historical* books implies that they were written by the earlier prophets, such as Samuel, Elijah, Elisha, or in the "schools of the prophets" which they founded and instructed.

Third Division, "The Writings."—After the return from the Captivity the spirit of prophecy died out. The worship of the people became formal, the religious teachers gave themselves to semi-philosophical and often profitless discussions. The warm, quick breath of the Lord no longer came with its burning message, which was to the prophet "as a fire shut up within his bones," so that he felt he *must* speak, and could not stay. And as this melancholy fact came to be recognized by the Jews, it was natural that they should value more highly what remained to them from their fathers of this legacy of Divine inspiration. The time for the close of the Old Testament Canon had come, and it was completed by the addition of a third division called the Hagiographa (Gk.), "Sacred Writings," or simply C'tubim (Heb.), "The Writings." It consisted of Ruth, Psalms, Job, Proverbs, Ecclesiastes, Song of Solomon, Lamentations, Daniel, Esther, Ezra, Nehemiah, Chronicles. We may take it that these books (some of them written about the time of Nehemiah, some at an earlier date) were brought together gradually by the Men of the Great Synagogue. We have not as much information as we should like about these men. But it seems most probable that they were an assembly of elders and scribes whom Ezra gathered round him, and engaged upon the work of collecting, transcribing, and, as we should say, "editing" the sacred books, and that they and their successors continued their labours from about 450 to 200 B.C. The persecution of Antiochus (B.C. 168) was the final crisis which stamped the sacred writings with their peculiar character. The king sought out "the books of the law," and burnt them; and the possession of a "book of the covenant" was a capital crime. According to common tradition it was this proscription of "the law" which led to the public reading of "the prophets" in the synagogues, an honour previously given only to the first division of the Canon. Undoubtedly the effect of the persecution was to direct more attention to the books connected with the foundation of their faith. The books of the third division were not at first regarded with the same veneration as the two former, and the right of some of them to a place in the Canon was long disputed by the rabbis, *e.g.* the books of Esther and Solomon's Song, neither of which contain the name of God.

The Synod of Jamnia, A.D. 90, finally fixed the Canon of the Old Testament as we have it in our Bibles, though, with the exception of two or three books, it had been virtually settled long before. Josephus about the same date writes: "We have not an innumerable multitude of books among us as the Greeks have, but only twenty-two books,* which contain the record of all past times, which are justly believed to be Divine. And of them five belong to Moses, which contain his laws and the traditions of the origin of mankind until his death. But as to the time from the death of Moses to the reign of Artaxerxes, King of Persia, the prophets who were after Moses wrote down what was done in their times in thirteen books. The remaining four books contain hymns to God and precepts for the conduct of human life . . . And how firmly we have given credit to these books of our own nation is evident by what we do; for during so many ages as have already passed, no one has been so bold as either to add anything to them, to take anything from them, or to make any change in them, but it becomes natural to all Jews . . . to esteem these books to contain Divine doctrines, to persist in them, and if occasion be, willingly to die for them" (Contra Apion, i. 8).

* Josephus reckons the number of the books at twenty-two, in order to make it accord with the number of letters in the Hebrew alphabet. This was a favourite practice with Jewish writers. According to common usage, Ruth was reckoned with Judges, as one book; the two books of Samuel, of Kings, of Chronicles, each as one; and the twelve minor prophets, Hosea, Joel, etc., to Malachi, as one book. There is no doubt that by the four books of "Hymns and Precepts," Josephus meant the Psalms, Proverbs, Ecclesiastes, and Solomon's Song. So that if we assume that he reckoned Ezra simply as a continuation of Chronicles, which it really is (compare last two verses of Chronicles with the first three of Ezra), his number will be thus made out—

Genesis, Exodus, Leviticus, Numbers, Deuteronomy	...	5
Psalms, Proverbs, Ecclesiastes, Solomon's Song ...	...	4
Joshua, Judges with Ruth		2
1 and 2 Samuel, 1 and 2 Kings, 1 and 2 Chronicles with Ezra		3
Nehemiah, Esther, Job		3
Isaiah, Jeremiah with Lamentations, Ezekiel, Daniel ...		4
The twelve minor prophets		1
		22

The last five rows (Joshua through minor prophets) are braced together as 13.

2. Canon of the New Testament.

The New Testament Canon, like the old, was formed gradually. There is little doubt that all the books which compose it were *in existence* before the close of the first century: but they were widely scattered over the Churches of Europe, Asia, and Africa. The Gospels would be first known in the circles in which they originated, the Pauline Epistles in the Churches to which they were addressed, and so with the other books. For reasons stated in the last chapter, a long time would necessarily elapse before all the twenty-seven books of the New Testament came to be universally known and recognized. Moreover, even where known, it was not natural that they should at once be placed on a level with the Canon of the Old Testament Scriptures. Those Scriptures had long been regarded with the utmost veneration as of Divine authority, the one sacred rule of faith and practice. It would in the first instance be impossible for the early Christians to regard these new works, written in their own age, as being worthy of the same veneration. Besides, as long as the apostles and their immediate disciples were living, it was natural that the Churches should look to *them* rather than to any written books for instruction in all matters relating to the Christian faith. But in the latter half of the second century these living witnesses had died out, heretical opinions were spreading, and treatises really spurious were being put forth under the cover of apostolic names. At this period, therefore, we find endeavours made to collect the genuine writings of the apostolic age; their unspeakable worth was more deeply felt, and a Canon of New Testament Scripture began to be formed. This was not done by any concerted action; nor was the result submitted to any general assembly; but by the labours of individual leaders in the Church, and the spontaneous and simultaneous action of many Churches in many places.

Earlier Portion.—We have evidence that about the year 170 A.D. there was a general recognition of a standard collection, or Canon, of New Testament Scriptures. Thus Dionysius of Corinth at that date, complaining that his own writings have been falsified, consoles himself with the reflection that "the same is done with the Scriptures of the Lord." The context shows that he is referring to the Gospels and Epistles, and he thus, by the distinctive title of the "Scriptures," puts them on a level of authority with the Old Testament. Theophilus of Antioch (A.D. 180), in like manner, puts the prophetic and the apostolic writings on a par; and so do other writers of the same period. Tertullian (A.D. 200) is the first who gives to the collection the title of the New Testament. What, then, did this early Canon contain? Beyond all dispute, the four Evangelists (Matthew, Mark, Luke, and John), the Book of Acts, the thirteen Epistles of Paul, the First Epistle of Peter, and the First of John. These writings were universally recognized in the Church from 170 onwards.

Later Additions.—The remaining seven books of our New Testament, viz. Hebrews, James, Second of Peter, Second and Third of John, Jude, and Revelation, secured more slowly a general acknowledgment. Thus Irenæus, Clement, and Tertullian (who all lived in the end of the second century), agree in acknowledging the Apocalypse; Irenæus adds the Second Epistle of John; Clement adds Hebrews, Second of John and Jude; Tertullian, the same: but these writings are placed by all three authors in a secondary place, along with some inferior works, such as the "Shepherd of Hermas," and the Epistle of Barnabas, which were ultimately excluded from the Canon. Throughout the third century we find the same uncertainty as to these seven books, some writers including some, and some others, in the Canon. Origen (A.D. 240) includes them all, though he mentions Jude, Second of Peter, Second and Third of John, as "controverted." The persecution of the Christians at the end of this century by Diocletian tended to make the distinction between canonical and uncanonical books more definite.* This emperor ordered the Christian Scriptures to be burned (A.D. 303), and this naturally pressed home for decision the question, what *are* the Christian Scriptures? The result was the inclusion of all the seven books in the Canon, and the exclusion of the apocryphal books that had sometimes been classed along with them. This appears to have been the decision of the Council of Laodicea (A.D. 363). For though, unfortunately, the list passed at that council is wanting in the original manuscript, Cyril of Jerusalem, who took part in it, gives in his catalogue of "Divine Scriptures" all our New Testament books except the Apocalypse; and Athanasius, Bishop of Alexandria, in his "festal epistle" of the same date (368), includes Revelation also. At the **Council of Carthage** (A.D. 397) it was determined that "besides the Canonical Scriptures nothing be read in the Church under the title of Divine Scriptures. The Canonical Scriptures are these: . . . of the New Testament four books of the Gospels, one book of the Acts of the Apostles, thirteen epistles of the Apostle Paul, one of the same (writer) to the Hebrews, two epistles of the Apostle Peter, three of John, one of James, one of Jude, and one book of the Apocalypse of John." So we have a clear enumeration of all the present contents of our New Testament, and of no other books, and they became the generally accepted Canon from that time forwards. The student should observe that their authority was not *given* to them by this council nor by any other. The decree just quoted goes on to say that it was passed for the purpose of *confirming the Canon received from the Fathers*. Not any formal council assigned to these books the position of authority they have so long preserved in the Church; they gained it by virtue of the Divine power which they exerted over the hearts of those who

* See Appendix B.

read them. They were placed in the Canon not simply because they were written by apostles or companions of apostles (for in one or two cases the authorship was doubtful), but because the truth they contained so enlightened the mind and touched the conscience as to produce an irresistible impression of its Divine origin. Hence it may truly be said, in the language of the old theologians, that the authority of Scripture is from God alone.

The following table, taken with some slight abridgment from Dr. Charteris's work, " Canonicity," may be studied as a supplement to this and the preceding chapter, showing the evidence for the authenticity and genuineness of the separate books, and how they gradually came to be recognized as part of the Canon. Observe that it does not follow that the writers in the left-hand column knew of *no other New Testament books* than those set against their names in the right-hand one. In many cases only a few fragments of their writings have come down to us. These contain quotations from or allusions to the books specified, but if we had their whole works, we might find in them references to many other books of the New Testament.

Writer.	Approximate Date.	New Testament Books used by him.
Barnabas	120 A.D.	Matt., Luke, John, Heb., 1 and 2 Tim.
Clement	90–100 A.D.	Matt., Mark, Luke, (indications of John and Acts), Rom., 1 Cor., Eph., 1 Tim., Tit., Heb., James, 1 Peter.
Ignatius	107–115 A.D.	Matt., John, 1 Cor., Eph., Phil., 1 Thess.
Polycarp	140–166 A.D.	Matt., Rom., 1 Cor., Gal., Eph., Phil., 1 and 2 Tim., 1 Peter, 1 John.
Papias	70–150 A.D.	Matt., Mark, 1 Peter, 1 John, Rev.
Basilides	125 A.D.	Matt., Luke, John, Romans, 1 and 2 Cor., Eph., Col., 1 Peter.

Writer.	Approximate Date.	New Testament Books used by him.
Marcion...	135–142 A.D.	Luke, Rom., 1 and 2 Cor., 1 and 2 Thess., Eph., Phil., Col., Philem.
Justin Martyr ...	139–148 A.D.	Four Gospels, Rev., Correspondence with Rom., 1 Cor., Col., 2 Thess., Heb.
Valentinus	140–160 A.D.	Matt., Luke, John, Rom., 1 Cor., Eph., Heb., 1 John.
Heracleon	Not later than 160 A.D.	Matt., Luke, John, Rom., 1 Cor., 2 Tim., (Commentary on John).
Ptolemæus	Ditto.	Matt., Mark, John, Rom., Cor., Gal., Eph., Col.
Tatian ...	170 A.D.	John certainly—and wrote "Diatessaron" which was probably a harmony of our four Gospels.
Athenagoras ...	177 A.D.	Matt., John, Rom., 1 and 2 Cor., Gal.
Theophilus	180–193 A.D.	Matt., Luke, John, Rom., 1 and 2 Cor., Eph., Phil., Col., 1 Tim., Tit., Heb., 1 Peter.
Syriac Version...	Second century.	All our New Testament *except* 2 Peter, 2 and 3 John, Jude, Rev.
Old Latin Version	Ditto.	All except Heb., 2 Peter, and (?) James.
Muratorian Canon	160–170 A.D.	All except Heb., James, and Peter.
Irenæus	140–202 A.D.	Four Gospels, Acts, 12 Epistles of Paul, 1 Peter, 1 and 2 John.
Clement of Alexandria	189–219 A.D.	All except James, 2 Pet., and 3 John.
Tertullian	160–220 A.D.	All except James, 2 Peter, and 3 John.
Origen ...	184–253 A.D.	All: though 2 Peter, 2 and 3 John doubtfully.
Dionysius of Alexandria	247–265 A.D.	All: but ascribes Rev. to another than John.
Eusebius ...	270–340 A.D.	Christian books in three classes. "Acknowledged:" four Gospels, Acts, all Epistles of Paul, 1 John, 1 Peter, Rev. "Disputed:" James, Jude, 2 Peter, 2 and 3 John. "Spurious:" Rev., according to some, along with many apocryphal writings.

Writer.	Approximate Date.	New Testament Books used by him.
Athanasius	329–373 A.D.	All as canonical.
Cyril of Jerusalem	Died 386 A.D.	All except Rev.
Epiphanius	367–403 A.D.	Canon exactly ours.
Chrysostom	Died 407 A.D.	All except 2 Peter, 2 and 3 John, Jude, Rev.
Augustine	354–430 A.D.	All, doubting authorship of Heb.
Jerome	329–420 A.D.	Canon exactly ours.
Council of Carthage	397 A.D.	Canon exactly ours.

CONTENTS AND CHARACTERISTICS OF THE CANONICAL BOOKS.

The contents of the Old Testament Canon may be roughly characterized as follows :—from Genesis to Esther inclusive, historical books; from Job to Solomon's Song, poetical; from Isaiah to Malachi, prophetic. This must not be confounded with the threefold division of the Jewish Canon already noticed. That proceeds upon a different principle; and the order of the books in the Hebrew Bible is different. The order of the books in our English Bible is that adopted in the Greek Version of the Old Testament (the Septuagint). The classification is based upon the style of composition—historic, poetic, prophetic. It is not a very good one, as many of the prophecies are couched in poetic form, and some portions of those books are historical. *Within* each division the order is chronological with one or two exceptions, which will be pointed out in due course.

The Pentateuch is the name given to the first five books of the Bible (Greek, *pente*, "five"). The Book of *Genesis* is so-called from the first word of the Bible in the original Hebrew, "In the beginning." *Genesis* is the Greek for "beginning." The name is also suitable to its contents. It relates to the beginnings of human history, and contains the lives of the early patriarchs down to their removal into Egypt. *Exodus* is the Greek word for "going out," and describes the escape of the Israelites from Egypt, the giving of the Law from Mount Sinai, and the erection of the tabernacle. *Leviticus* is so-called because it consists of Levitical ordinances—ordinances for the priestly tribe of Levi, either directions for their own observance or regulations which they were to see that the people observed. They may be thus classified: (1) laws about sacrifices, chaps. i.–vii.; (2) laws concerning purity, xi.–xvi.; (3) laws designed to separate Israel from other nations, xvii.–xx.; (4) laws concerning the priests, xxi., xxii.; (5) laws about holy days and festivals, xxiii.–xxv.; (6) laws about vows, xxvii. There is also a small historical section (viii.–x.) referring to the consecration of Aaron and his sons, and a prophetic chapter (xxvi.). The Book of *Numbers* takes up the history where it is left in Exodus; relates the advance of the children of Israel to the borders of the Promised Land, their repulse and subsequent wandering in the wilderness for thirty-eight years. The book derives its name from the two numberings of the people at the beginning and end of their wanderings. *Deuteronomy* is so-called from its name in the Septuagint, meaning the second law. It is a re-enactment of the Mosaic code, suited to the different condition of the people when settled down in the Promised Land. While fuller in ceremonial, and containing many additional enactments, it is in many respects a mitigation and softening down of the severity of the first legislation, sacrifices being appointed for some things which under the old law were punishable by death, and cities of refuge being provided for unintentional homicides. The book concludes with the last blessing and death of Moses.

The Books of **Joshua and Judges** relate the invasion and partial conquest of Canaan. Joshua has been called the Domesday Book of the Israelites; but it must be understood that the division and apportionment of the land which it records was prospective. Most of the country was still in the hands of their enemies, and had to be won from them " with the sword and with the bow." During the unsettled period which intervened between Joshua and Samuel, there arose a succession of chieftains who obtained more or less extensive victories over the Philistines and other inhabitants of the land, and who bore sway over their own tribe and the immediately surrounding district. These chieftains are known in history as the "Judges," and their exploits are recorded in the book that bears that name. The sweet story of *Ruth* refers to this period, but it was not written till a much later date.

The Books of **Samuel, Kings, and Chronicles** contain the history of the Israelites from the establishment of the monarchy down to its ending in the Captivity. They are based on other historical books which have unhappily perished; but to which they make frequent reference, such as "the Book of Jasher," "the Chronicles of King David," "the Book of Nathan the Prophet," "the Book of Gad the Seer," "the Book of the Acts of Solomon," "the Book of the Chronicles of the Kings of Israel," and the "Book of the Chronicles of the Kings of Judah" (not to be confounded with the existing Books of Chronicles). Many of these were, no doubt, contemporary records or annals, and supplied the historian of these books with reliable information. The Books of Samuel and Kings exhibit great literary skill, particularly the former. Nothing can exceed the graphic power of the narratives in "Samuel," which makes them a constant source of delight to a juvenile audience. The earlier portion of the Kings is very little inferior; but the account of the later reigns is more condensed, and only occasionally gives that fulness of incident which is supplied to us in the reigns of Saul and David. The same is true in a still greater degree of the *Chronicles*. The First Book of Chronicles consists chiefly of genealogical tables. The Second Book of Chronicles covers the same period as the two Books of Kings, but it refers only to the Kings of Judah. The kingdom of Israel is ignored, except during the brief period of its alliance with Judah. Many incidents recorded in the Kings are omitted, and several additional ones reported; but in other cases the same events are related in almost the very same words in Kings and in Chronicles, showing that both writers have drawn from a common source. The author of the latter quotes at least a dozen authorities which he mentions by name. He also gives many genealogies copied from the registers, not elsewhere found in the Bible. The Chronicles were written later than the Kings, though the history they contain does not come down any later, except in the last two verses. These are identical with the first two and a half of Ezra, and it is by some supposed that Ezra wrote both books, originally intending them as one volume.

Ezra, Nehemiah, and Esther. *Ezra* records the decree of Cyrus for the restoration of the temple, the first return of the Jews from captivity under Prince Zerubbabel, and the erection of the second temple; also the return of Ezra himself with another band of exiles, 458 B.C. *Nehemiah* tells how he rebuilt the walls of Jerusalem, and re-established the ancient religion. His book contains many graphic pictures, and deserves more frequent perusal than it usually gets. The Book of *Esther* contains an episode in the history of the exiled Jews, which followed closely on the time of Nehemiah, if it did not precede it. It contains no direct reference to religion, but points indirectly towards God's care for his chosen people, and affords many excellent moral lessons.

The Book of **Job** presents, in dramatic form, a discussion of the problem, Why is evil suffered to befall the righteous? Job's three friends would meet the difficulty by denying the fact. They hold fast to the old theory which Christ himself rebukes (for it was still current in His day), that if a man is specially afflicted it is because of special sin. They will have it that Job is not righteous, *or else* such suffering would not have befallen. Job holds fast his integrity, but sees no solution of the problem. The true answer is to be gathered partly from the prologue (chaps. i. and ii.) and the epilogue (xlii.), and partly from the speeches of Elihu and the Lord Himself at the end of the book, viz. that so far as the righteous man himself is concerned, it is a test of his fidelity, which, if it stands the strain, will hereafter be amply rewarded; that as regards God, the patience of the righteous under suffering is a tribute to His glory, an answer to His adversaries; but, further, that the man and his life are but a very small part of the vast God-governed universe, and that he must not expect to understand fully the connection of this little part with the great whole, but submit himself to the infinite wisdom and righteousness of God, in confidence that the Judge of all the earth will do right. The scene of this drama is the land of Uz; the time is difficult to determine, since it makes no reference to the history of the Covenant people. It may be even prior to Moses; but many considerations combine to show that the book itself was not written before the Exile. It contains some of the most magnificent poetry in the Old Testament (see especially chaps. xxviii. and xxxviii.), but its beauty is much obscured by the bad translation of our Authorized Version, which, it is to be hoped, the Revised Version now in progress will greatly amend.

The **Psalms** are a collection of sacred poetry gradually compiled between the time of Moses and the close of the Old Testament Canon. One, at least, is ascribed to the great Lawgiver; many others are undoubtedly by David; the authorship of the greater number is unknown, the superscriptions in our English Bible being a later addition not to be relied on. Nor is the question of great importance. The Holy Spirit witnesses to His own work in these sublime and pathetic utterances. Should any one question it, let him produce from the whole range of the world's literature prior to Christ, a sacred poem which makes the faintest approach to such Psalms as the 23rd, the 25th, the 103rd, either in the mingled grandeur and tenderness of their conception of God, or the loving trustful fellowship with Him to which the writers have attained.*

The **Proverbs** are a collection of moral and religious maxims, of which Solomon's collection formed the nucleus. In their own sphere they are as superior as the Psalms to anything of like character in the literature of other nations. By their truth and pungency many of them have become as "familiar as household words," even in circles where their source is utterly forgotten.

The Book of **Ecclesiastes** appears to be written with a view of showing the unsatisfactory nature of all earthly sources of delight, and leads up to the practical conclusion, "Fear God, and keep His commandments." It presents many difficulties both as to its authorship and interpretation, to which the best key will be found in Dr. Plumptre's "Ecclesiastes" (Cambridge Bible for Schools).

Solomon's Song is of the nature of a dialogue between two lovers, and there is a chorus of "Daughters of Jerusalem," who from time to time join in it. Many commentators have seen in it a mystical allusion to Christ and His bride, the Church.

Isaiah, Jeremiah, Ezekiel, and Daniel, are commonly classified together as the Greater Prophets. They stand in chronological order. *Isaiah* was the earliest. He prophesied during the reigns of Uzziah, Jotham, Ahaz, and Hezekiah. His book is divided into two sections by the interposition of the historical chapters, xxxvi.–xxxix.

---

* Concerning difficulties in some of the Psalms, see chap. iv. of this book.

between the prophecies proper. Some critics have assigned the latter section, xl.–lxvi., to a writer of a hundred and fifty years later date, chiefly on account of the mention of Cyrus *by name* so many years before he lived, which is certainly an unwonted occurrence in Scripture prophecy; but the language and style are the same throughout, and so far point to the same author for both portions. He has been called the *Evangelical* prophet, not only because of his Messianic predictions and the prophecy of the ingathering of the Gentiles, but on account of the *tone* of his writings, which reminds us of the Gospel in its earnest pleading with sinners, its broad promises of free forgiveness, and its sublime pathos.

Jeremiah has been called the "weeping prophet." He saw the long-threatened judgments of the Lord fall upon his nation, living in the reigns of Jehoiakim and Zedekiah, when Judah was carried into captivity. His prophecies are mingled with history which recounts the bitter opposition and persecution which he endured at the hands of his adversaries in Jerusalem. His prophecies refer chiefly to the Covenant people, but the latter chapters of his book foretell the fate of Egypt, Philistia, Moab, Ammon, Edom, Damascus, Kedar, and Elam. As in Isaiah, there are overtures of mercy from the God who says, "I am a Father to Israel, and Ephraim is my first-born," and a few hopeful glimpses into the future. But the tone of mourning, reproof, and denunciation prevails, and he weeps for "the sins of the daughter of his people." The Book of *Lamentations* which follows is in the same strain.

Ezekiel was a contemporary of Jeremiah, though younger than he. He was one of the leading Jews carried away from Jerusalem along with King Jehoiachin by Nebuchadnezzar, and he prophesied among his captive countrymen by the river Chebar, in Babylon. A chief characteristic of Ezekiel's writings is their apocalyptic or visionary nature. In this respect they resemble Daniel, Zechariah, and the Revelation of St. John. A great portion is eminently evangelical, and yet awaits its fulfilment in the Church of Christ.

Daniel was taken captive in the third year of Jehoiakim, and rose to eminence in the court of Babylon. The book is partly historic and partly prophetic. The latter portion distinctly predicts the death of "Messiah," that name for the coming Saviour first occurring here.

The **Twelve Minor Prophets** are those which close the Old Testament Canon from Hosea to Malachi inclusive. *Hosea*, *Joel*, and *Amos* were contemporary with Isaiah; so was *Micah*, though younger. *Jonah* probably lived earlier (see 2 Kings xiv. 25). The dates of *Obadiah*, *Nahum*, and *Habakkuk* cannot be assigned with any certainty, but they seem to have preceded *Zephaniah*, who prophesied in the reign of King Josiah. *Haggai*, *Zechariah*, and *Malachi* executed their mission after the return from the Captivity, the latest being contemporary with Nehemiah. Thus the Minor Prophets extend over a space of four hundred years, nearly equal to that from Chaucer to Wordsworth. The limits of this work will not allow us to characterize them separately. Their writings are perplexing to the ordinary reader from reference to places, persons, and circumstances with which he is not acquainted; but with the aid of a good commentary they will repay careful study. Joel, Amos, and Habakkuk in particular abound in splendid imagery, and clear enunciation of important truths. In the last-named prophet is found the maxim, "The just shall live by faith," which Paul quotes three times, and which Luther made the keystone of his theology.

We now advance to the books of the New Testament, which we shall treat rather more fully.

The Gospels give us four accounts of the life of Christ on earth. They are all of them more or less fragmentary. None of them keep strictly to the chronological order of events. Similar incidents and similar utterances of Christ are frequently placed together, though they actually occurred at different times. John observes the order of time more closely than the others. The first three Gospels are called the *synoptic* Gospels, from a Greek word which signifies "seeing together." They look at Christ's life from the same point of view, and to a large extent report the same incidents and discourses. The fourth Gospel was written last, and forms a sort of supplement to the others, and tells us much that they have omitted. The three synoptic Gospels present the following characteristic features in comparison with the fourth. They present more prominently the *humanity* of Christ; John keeps His *divinity* more in the foreground. They are concerned most with His ministry in *Galilee*, only referring indirectly to Christ's visits to Jerusalem prior to the crucifixion. John reports these fully, and says comparatively little about the life in Galilee. The synoptics report more of Christ's *miracles* and *parables;* John gives us more of His *longer discourses*. The discourses reported in the synoptics are concerned chiefly with *human duties*, and the events connected with the destruction of Jerusalem and the last days; those in the fourth tell us more about the *person of Christ* Himself, His relation to His heavenly Father on the one hand, and to His disciples on the other. Hence, roughly speaking, the tone of the synoptics is more *moral*, that of John more *spiritual*. Among the three synoptic Gospels Matthew and Mark have most in common. The narrative in Mark's Gospel, though the shortest, is distinguished by many little graphic touches not found in the others, such as the multitude sitting on the "green grass," the frequent reference to Christ's "turning and looking upon his disciples," etc. It has also two very vividly described miracles (vii. 31–37; viii. 22–26) peculiar to itself. These are probably due to Peter's keen observation; for it was (according to tradition) under his instruction that Mark wrote. Still, if the teacher were selecting one Gospel for lessons in his class, we should suggest Luke's, on account of the greater fulness of incident and the many beautiful parables which are found in it alone. It was probably the last written of the three synoptic Gospels. It has been said that Matthew's Gospel was written chiefly for Jews; Luke's chiefly for Gentiles; Mark's for all without distinction. Matthew and Luke alone give us any informtion about the birth of Christ and His early years. All four Gospels relate the crucifixion and resurrection, and likewise the miracle of the feeding of the five thousand. We gain much by these four independent accounts of Christ's ministry, each written from its own standpoint. Not only is there a confirmation of testimony for those events which they relate in common; but we have the same advantage in endeavouring to picture to ourselves what manner of person Christ was, that is given us when we gather our idea of some one whom we have never seen, from four photographs taken from four different points of view. We catch different aspects of the features, different expressions of the countenance; and our idea of the person is clearer and fuller than if it had been gained from a single portraiture.

"The Acts of the Apostles."—This book was evidently compiled by the author of the third Gospel (compare Acts i. 1 with Luke i. 3). It covers a period of a little more than thirty years, A.D. 30–62. The design of the writer was to record the fulfilment of Christ's promise to send the Holy Spirit, and the consequent spreading of the Gospel among Jews and Gentiles. The earlier portion of the book relates the descent of the Spirit, and the first preaching of the Gospel by the twelve and their immediate associates in Jerusalem—Stephen, Philip, etc. It also narrates the conversion of Paul. The latter part of the book, ch. xiii. to the end, attaches itself almost exclusively to him, and follows him to his imprisonment in Rome, where it leaves him, ending somewhat abruptly. The writer was evidently *with* Paul in those portions of his narrative where he says "we" did thus and thus; and the description given in these parts is especially vivid. See in particular the account of the shipwreck, ch. xxvii., where the details are in exact harmony with all we know of the principles and methods of navigation in ancient times.

The thirteen **Epistles of Paul** (Romans to Philemon inclusive) constitute the chief portion of the remainder of the New Testament, and enable us to form a clearer idea of the great apostle of the Gentiles than of any other character in the Bible. His writings are more argumentative than any other portion of the sacred volume. The correspondence between them and what we learn of Paul in the Acts has already been indicated; likewise the general resemblance of style and identity of authorship of the letters themselves. But the style differs considerably, according to the persons to whom it was addressed and the special purpose of the writer. The Epistle to the *Romans* approaches more nearly than any other to a systematic theological treatise. Paul begins by showing the need of the Gospel, first for Gentiles, on account of universal human depravity, and then for Jews, because the law had proved an insufficient remedy; next he unfolds the remedy provided in Christ, and how faith in Him secures peace with God, and ushers the believer into a new life. This portion of his argument culminates in the eighth chapter with its grand climax, "Who shall separate us from the love of Christ?" In chapters ix., x., and xi. he deals with the difficult problem suggested by Israel's rejection of the Gospel, and occupies the remainder of his letter with the enforcement of those practical duties to which genuine faith will lead. The scope of the Epistles to the *Corinthians*, and their bearing on our Church life of to-day, has been already sufficiently indicated in our preceding chapter. The Epistle to the *Galatians* was written to the Churches of Galatia which Paul had founded. After his departure, certain teachers of the Judaizing party in the early Christian Church persuaded his Gentile converts that, though faith in Christ was well enough as far as it went, yet, if they would be perfect in God's sight, they must be circumcised and keep the law of Moses. Paul writes in warm indignation to reclaim them from this error, and the Epistle is an armoury of weapons against the Ritualism so rife in the present day, which, in the importance it attaches to forms and ceremonies, presents a close resemblance to the tenets of the Judaizing party. The Epistles to *Ephesians* and *Colossians* were evidently written at the same time, and to Churches in the same neighbourhood. The line of thought is the same in both, and often there is a very close verbal resemblance. Their object is to set forth the growth of the Church, especially in relation to its Divine Head; and they both conclude with certain practical exhortations to husbands and wives, parents and children, masters and servants. The Epistle to the *Philippians* is a letter to Paul's favourite Church, thanking them for a present, congratulating them on their steadfast faith, warning them against the Judaizing teachers, and showing from his own experience what complete emancipation from the law is obtained by faith in Christ. The Epistles to the *Thessalonians* have for their distinguishing feature the frequent reference to the "coming of the Lord." The Church at Thessalonica appears to have understood from the First Epistle that the "day of the Lord" was immediately at hand or had even already come (see 2 Thess. ii. 2, Revised Version), and thereupon some left off working, and wasted their time in idle dreams and discussions. The second letter is written to correct the false impression and the consequent misconduct. These are considered by most critics to be the earliest of Paul's Epistles, and Dr. Stanley Leathes thinks that this may account for the expectation of a very early return of Christ which Paul evidently then had, and for the "allusions to be found in these Epistles, which in the later ones are less frequent, as the writer became more familiar with the truth of Christ (John xvi. 13)." The Epistles to *Timothy* and *Titus* are called the "pastoral Epistles," because they were written for the guidance of these two younger brethren in the pastoral oversight of the Churches. Second of Timothy is the latest of the Pauline Epistles, and contains a touching allusion to his approaching martyrdom (iv. 6–8). *Philemon*, see later on (page 69).

The Epistle to the **Hebrews** is by some writers ascribed to Paul; by others to Barnabas or Apollos. It was written to dissuade *Jewish Christians* who were exposed to trials of various kinds from falling back and renouncing the faith of Christ. The writer therefore labours to prove the superiority of the New Covenant to the Old, by showing from "the Scriptures" the superiority of Jesus to the High Priests, and the transitory and inefficient nature of the provisions of the Old Law.

The Catholic Epistles is a name frequently given to the six last Epistles of the New Testament, because they are written to Christians in general, without any distinction of race or Church, that being the proper meaning of the word "catholic." The Epistle of *James* was written not by the son of Zebedee, but by "the brother of our Lord," mentioned in Gal. i. 19, Acts xii. 17, xv. 13, xxi. 18, who was possibly, but by no means certainly, identical with "James the son of Alphæus" (Matt. x. 3). His Epistle is the least theological of any, but eminently practical. It would appear that Paul's doctrine of justification by faith had been so misunderstood and misapplied by some people, that they thought they should be saved by a mere intellectual assent to the truths of the gospel. James assures them that that kind of faith would save no man. " The faith that is without works is dead." He also reproves the sins of the tongue, the oppression of the poor, cringing subserviency to the rich, and other failings, and strengthens the brethren under persecution. The *First Epistle of Peter* is also largely directed to comfort believers under the trials they had to pass through. It glows with fervour, and its tone is just what we should have expected from this apostle. The *Second Epistle of Peter* and *Jude* present such close similarity that some have thought the one was copied from the other. The Epistles of *John* are eminently characteristic; not, indeed, of the John as mediæval painters depict him, but as he really appears in the pages of the New Testament and in the traditions of the Church—"a son of thunder," a warm-hearted, enthusiastic, sincere, loving man, who in the vehemence of his love will say and do strong things. His Epistles abound in short pregnant utterances, expressing truth in its most forcible form. He ever sets before his eyes an ideal, and rejects everything that comes short of it (see First Epistle, ii. 15; iii. 6; iv. 18, etc.). "Deeds, not words," is his motto. He has a special abhorrence of anything like insincerity—mere empty profession (see ii. 4, 9; iii. 7, 17, 18; iv. 20, etc.).

The **Revelation**, or *Apocalypse*, is also by the Apostle John. It was probably written prior to the destruction of Jerusalem, A.D. 70; but is by some writers assigned to the reign of Domitian, about A.D. 96. The book is full of gorgeous imagery, derived chiefly from the writings of Isaiah, Ezekiel, and Daniel, and from the ritual of the temple. The name, Apocalypse (Greek), or Revelation (Latin), signifies "unveiling;" but as to what is "unveiled" commentators are by no means agreed. According to one school of interpreters the book consists of prophecies already fulfilled; according to a second, it sketches prophetically the whole history of the Church, from the age of the apostles to the consummation of all things; a third maintains that all its prophecies refer to a yet future period not yet commenced; while a fourth holds that it contains no prediction at all regarding events and persons, but is an allegorical representation of certain warring tendencies and principles. The commentators of these different schools are again divided among themselves as to the interpretation of the several parts. Under these circumstances we would strongly advise the Sunday school teacher to defer the question of the interpretation of the Apocalypse until he is quite sure he understands all the rest of the Bible.

WORKS FOR REFERENCE AND FURTHER STUDY.

The article "Canon" in Smith's "Bible Dictionary."
The article "Canon" in the "Encyclopædia Britannica."
The article "Canon" in the "Religious Cyclopædia." Edited by Dr. Schaff.
"Help to the Reading of the Bible." By Dr. Nicholls. $1.00.
"History of the Canon of the New Testament." By Canon Westcott. Macmillan. (For the advanced student.) $3.00.
Bleek's "Introduction to the Study of the Old Testament." T. T. Clark. (For the advanced student.) $4.00.
Bleek's "Introduction to the Study of the New Testament.' T. T. Clark. (For the advanced student.) $6.00.

CHAPTER III.

ON THE LANGUAGE AND STYLE OF SCRIPTURE—THE BIBLE A UNIQUE BOOK.

The language and style of Scripture are not uniform throughout. They vary considerably in the different books. It could not be otherwise. For, as we have seen, "the Scripture" is a collection of sixty-six books, or treatises, written by about forty different authors, the earliest of whom is separated from the latest by an interval of at least a thousand years. The books of the Old Testament were written in Hebrew (the later ones in the Chaldee dialect); the books of the New Testament in Greek. These books, moreover, differ in their subject-matter, and in the form of composition adopted. Nearly every known form of literary composition is to be found within the covers of the Bible. We have history, biography, autobiography, legal codes, compressed annals and registers, lyric and dramatic poetry, prophecies and visions, letters private and public, didactic treatises, collections of pithy sayings, etc. Now, the Spirit, under whose influence the books were written, did not so control the authors' minds as to make them either write in a dialect of which they had no previous knowledge, or in a style which was in any way unnatural to them. The peculiarities of the author's individual temperament and cast of thought are clearly discernible in nearly every case, as also his diction. Mark does not write like John, nor Peter like

Paul. Yet, notwithstanding all these differences, there are many points of resemblance, which constitute what may be roughly termed "the language and style of Scripture," and which, even apart from any distinct recollection of the words, enable us at once to recognize an extract from the Bible when we hear it, or to say with confidence of a passage taken from any other book, "That is not in the Bible." No doubt this is in part owing to the fact that what we commonly call "the Bible" is a translation of the sixty-six books of Scripture into one language —a translation finally revised and moulded by just two scholars; so that there is a distinctive unity in the English Bible above what belongs to the original Scripture. But notwithstanding this, even if the Scriptures be read in the languages in which they were first written, there are certain characteristics peculiar to them which mark out the book as a whole, and place it in strong contrast to the sacred books of most other religions. These characteristics are more strongly marked in some portions of Scripture than in others, and they concern the matter as well as the language and style of Scripture. The Sunday school teacher should note the following :—

1. **Dignity.**—Wherever you open the Bible, you find a style and treatment which impresses you with a sense of solemnity, and even majesty. There is nothing trivial, nothing flippant, nothing frivolous. The little story of Ruth—as simple and natural as any tale could well be— still carries this mark upon it. The brief letter in which Paul requests Philemon to pardon his runaway slave is as full of dignity as it is of tenderness, as rich and devout in tone (though it deals with a practical incident of common life) as his letters to the Churches on doctrinal subjects, or his pastoral Epistles to Timothy and Titus. Take up one of the *Apocryphal* books, such as the story of Tobias and his dog, or Bel and the Dragon, and compare it with the books of the Old Testament, which they were intended

to imitate; or take up the so-called "Gospel of Thomas," with its stories of the Child Jesus learning his letters, making the clay sparrows fly, and carrying water in his cloak, and compare it with Luke's brief account of Christ's boyhood, and you feel at once the difference between the dignity of our canonical Scriptures and the triviality of these apocryphal productions.

2. **Reference throughout to God and Righteousness.**—The dignity which pervades the whole of the Bible is largely due to the fact that all its writers have this one end in view: to declare the will and works of God, the will and works that "make for righteousness." This makes the history, the biography, the poetry of the Bible differ from all other history, biography, and poetry. If the Bible tells the story of Creation, it is not that it may give us some useful information in physical science, but that it may present before us in the most striking way God as the Author of all that is, and as the Father and the Friend of man, ordering all things for his good. If the Bible gives us a history of the Jews, it is not that it may exalt them as a nation and extol their deeds, nor that it may supply a missing page in the general volume of ancient history; but that it may show how God singled them out for His own purposes, that He might train them in righteousness, exhibit before the world His character as a God at once holy and merciful, and by His dealings with this chosen people prepare the way for the coming of His Son, to set up the kingdom of everlasting righteousness. If the Bible contains many interesting biographies, it is not that the fame of these individuals may be perpetuated, but that in their lives the truths that pertain to righteousness and the will of God may be set before us in living characters. So both in the story of individual and national life, it is God and His law that are made prominent all through. Prosperity and adversity are represented as coming from Him; His hand is seen in the great things

and the small; the righteous God rules. So with the Psalms; so with the books of the Prophets. Their main function is not to predict events, but to bear witness for God and righteousness. Even the Messianic prophecies will be found to have their root in this conviction, divinely wrought in the prophet's breast, that God's righteous will must triumph, evil must be overcome by good, the righteous Seed of the woman must at last bruise the serpent's head, if not in the person of Israel as a whole, in the person of some kingly representative; if not by Judah, yet by a righteous "remnant;" if even that "remnant" fails, still by "the Servant of the Lord," His will shall be done, evil shall be trodden out, righteousness shall triumph, the kingdom of heaven (the kingship of God) be established on earth. Hence the enormous difference between the prophecies of Scripture and the utterances of the oracles of heathen nations. They (whether true or false) were all *particular*, referring to certain persons or events for limited and temporary ends; but these all bear upon the accomplishment of the will of God and His law of everlasting righteousness. We need not point out how still more abundantly this is true of the writings of the New Testament. From first to last the Bible is the Book of God—the Book of Righteousness. The language and style are in harmony with the subject-matter and the main aim of the book. They give it a character of its own, evinced further in the features we go on to describe, most of them traceable to this same fundamental fact as their cause and origin.

3. **Suppression of the Personality of the Writers.**—What Dr. Campbell says of the Gospels is true of almost every book in the Bible: "The subject of the narrative so engrosses the attention of the writer that he is himself as nobody, and is quite forgotten by the reader, who is never led by the tenour of the narration so much as even to think of him. He introduces nothing as from himself.

We have no opinions of his; no remarks, conjectures, doubts, inferences; no reasonings about the causes or effects of what is related." The same applies to all the historical portions of Scripture, to all the catholic Epistles, and to most of the prophetical books. The thought of God seems so to overshadow the writer, that his own personality disappears. When we take up other biographies and narrative treatises we commonly find the author intruding himself in one way or another, with more or less conspicuousness; our attention is drawn from the subject to think about the writer, either with approval or disapproval, as the case may be; but in reading the history of David, or the story of Ruth, or the life of Christ, or the Acts of the Apostles, no one ever thinks of the author, or would ever ask, "Who wrote this book?" if that question were not forced upon him by other considerations. It may seem that the Book of Nehemiah and the Epistles of Paul are glaring exceptions. They *are* exceptions, but they are of the kind that prove the rule. The Book of Nehemiah being in the form of an autobiography, it was simply impossible, from the nature of the case, that the personal pronoun should be kept out; but this constantly recurring "I" strikes us as something altogether strange and unexampled in our reading of the Bible; and by its strangeness shows how general in the other parts of the Old Testament is the suppression of the writer's person. Paul's Epistles are letters written to individuals and Churches in whom he had a deep personal interest, and with most of whom he had been in close personal connection. To have excluded from these letters all friendly greetings, all allusions to their past intimacy, would have been most unnatural, and would have made the letters less effective for the purpose for which they were written. But nothing shows more clearly how far the *personal* element is kept in the background than the fact that many Sunday school teachers read these Epistles without ever realizing that they are the letters of a pastor to his flock or to his personal friend. So completely does the Divine element—the power that makes for righteousness—predominate over every other, that the less thoughtful reader overlooks the personal human element altogether, and sees nothing there except teaching sent from God, instruction in the way of holiness.

4. Impartiality and Candour.—If the biographers and historians of Scripture suppress *themselves*, they do not suppress *facts;* and the one feature is as unique and remarkable as the other. Outside the sacred volume we hardly ever find a national historian who can resist the temptation to suppress or gloss over facts that are discreditable to his nation; and in like manner with the biographer, that which is dishonourable to his hero is either omitted or palliated, extenuated, and explained away; while, on the other hand, the enemies of the nation or the hero rarely get fair treatment. The Bible histories and biographies present a remarkable contrast in this respect. The narrative proceeds with the utmost candour and impartiality. The vices, the transgressions, the defeats and reverses of the chosen people are set down just as plainly and frankly as their virtues, their obedience, their victories and successes. The sins and shortcomings of Jacob, Samuel, David, and Peter are disclosed in the impartial narrative of their lives, without the slightest attempt to excuse or justify them. On the other hand, the generosity of Esau's disposition is displayed as fully and frankly as his impetuosity and lightmindedness; the redeeming features of Saul's character are set forth just as plainly as his faults; the magnanimous and chivalrous confidence shown by the Philistine King Achish towards David stands out in contrast with the latter's duplicity and treachery; and in the gospel narrative the Samaritan, the Syrophenician, the Greek, and the Roman compare to advantage with the Jews whose path they cross. The evil in good men, the goodness in bad men is brought to light with the most absolute candour. From first to last there is an openness, a straightforwardness, a transparent truthfulness, which we should vainly look for to an equal degree in any other book.

5. **Dramatic Style.**—The distinguishing feature of the drama is that it places men and women upon the stage where they speak and act in the presence of the spectators who from their speech and action *infer* their character and gather up the story. There is no description given of them, no analysis of their motives, no comment on their proceedings; there they are, and what they say and do tells its own tale. Now this is one of the most remarkable features of the Scripture narrative. The inspired writers place the men and women before us, report their deeds and words, almost without note or comment, and leave us to judge of them. There is no panegyric on the noble deeds of good men, no invective against the evil practices of bad men. The writer utters no exclamation of delight at the former, no exclamation of horror over the latter. Even where we should most expect some such expression of feeling, it is absent. Not even over the men who conspired to crucify our Saviour is there any outburst of indignation. No observations are offered on the most tragic scene in the world's history. The facts are left to speak for themselves. In like manner with the actors in that scene, and with the other personages who cross the stage of Scripture history: there is no elaborate description of their character, and yet how vividly that character stands out before us! We almost seem to have known Laban and Jacob, David and Jonathan, Peter and Thomas, by personal acquaintance. *We* could describe their character, but the Scripture writers have not done so. To take the last two as examples. The evangelists do not tell us, "Peter was a warm-hearted, impulsive man, capable of strong personal attachment, but liable to sudden changes of feeling, at

times bold even to rashness, and at other times unaccountably overcome with panic." Or, "Thomas was a man who always looked on the dark side of things, who could never believe what he wanted to believe, a man who could be strong with the courage of despair, but never confident with the cheerfulness of hope." Not a word of any such description in the Gospels; only a few incidents and sayings reported (only three in the case of Thomas), and yet the two men stand before us as though they were alive in our midst. Their character is perfectly displayed, but it is displayed dramatically, by their own speech and action.

6. **Simplicity and Sobriety.**—Though the style of Scripture is dramatic, it is remarkably simple and sober. There is no straining after effect, no pompous declamation, no endeavour to astonish, no note of exclamation over the wonderful things recorded. The greatest miracles of the Old Testament and the New are related as simply and unostentatiously as though they were ordinary occurrences. Most writers who had such things to record would have expatiated on the wondrous power displayed. The utmost that the writers of Scripture say is, "The people were astonished, and glorified God;" or, "They marvelled greatly." Even these observations (be it remarked) are observations of the *people*, the writer simply reporting what he heard and saw; and more often even *they* are absent; the mighty deeds, the awful judgments, the signal mercies of God, are quietly narrated without enlarging or expatiating on them in any way. Nor can we forbear to note in passing, that in these mighty deeds themselves there is always a certain simplicity and reasonableness. There is a certain proportion between the power displayed and the end to be accomplished. There is none of the wild extravagance which we find in the religious books of other Eastern nations. Compare, for instance, with the Gospel narratives of Christ's boyhood and subsequent miracles

the prodigies related of Buddha: such as his being tied, when he was a baby, to a large mortar, which he pulled till it became wedged between two large trees, and then dragging it further, tore up the trees by the roots; or of his turning the hairs of his body into hundreds of wolves to terrify the villages; or of his cutting off the hair of his head, and throwing it into the air, where it remained suspended at a height of sixteen miles, like a beautiful bird;—and the contrast with the simplicity and sobriety of the Scripture record will be at once apparent.* The *language*, and style of *composition*, is for the most part exceedingly simple, almost the only exception being a few of the Epistles. No doubt there are other portions of the Bible which it is not easy to understand; as, for instance, the Book of Job and some of the prophets. But the difficulty arises either from the profundity of the subject treated of, or from our ignorance of the precise situation of the writer and the circumstances to which he incidentally alludes, or from defects in the translation; not from any obscurity in the language employed. He that runs may read it. Teachers of foreign languages have found, when they wished to exercise their pupil's first efforts in the translation of some book, there was no book so simple as the books of the Bible. The Gospel of John is probably (so far as *language* is concerned) the simplest book ever written for grown-up persons.

7. **Figurative Speech.**—In common with other oriental literature, the language of the Bible is rich in metaphors, similes, and all kinds of figurative speech. The Eastern

---

* The following is literally translated from the Vishnu Purana, a Hindoo sacred book: "Having thus spoken, the mighty Makerwara created from his mouth a being with a thousand heads, a thousand eyes, and a thousand feet, wielding a thousand clubs and a thousand shafts." . . . This being "then created, from the pores of his skin, powerful demigods, the mighty attendants upon Rudra, of equal valour and strength, who started by hundreds and thousands into existence." The portion omitted is a long paragraph expatiating on the terrific powers of this being.

mind delights in such comparisons, and they are characteristic of other Eastern books as well as the Bible. But most Sunday school teachers will be struck with the prevalence of this feature in the Bible as compared with books of their ordinary reading. They lend great force and vividness to the style, but to the English reader they are sometimes a little perplexing. He can appreciate the beauty of our Lord's parables, and the splendid images that brighten the poetry of the Psalms—such as the sun coming out of his chamber clad as a bridegroom, and rejoicing as a strong man to run a race, or the Lord leading his people like a shepherd his flock. He can see the meaning of the strong description of the emptying of Jerusalem bare of all men and treasures, "And I will wipe Jerusalem as a man wipeth a dish; wiping it and turning it upside down;" but when he reads in Isaiah's prophecy (lx. 5–9) of the restoration of Jerusalem, "The forces of the Gentiles shall come unto thee. The multitude of camels shall cover thee, the dromedaries of Midian and Ephah; . . . and all the flocks of Kedar shall be gathered unto thee, the rams of Nebaioth shall minister unto thee," etc., he may not see, at first sight, that these animals are put by a figure of speech for their masters, the travelling merchants and shepherd tribes of Arabia. Nor may he at once see in the following words—"Who are these that fly as a cloud, and as the doves to their windows? Surely the isles shall wait for me,"—the beautiful picture of the fleet of ships from distant lands drawing near to the shores of Palestine, in the distance like a cloud on the horizon, and as they come nearer their white sails glimmering in the sun like the wings of flying doves.

Another common oriental figure which may sometimes mislead the reader, is what the rhetoricians term "hyperbole," when a writer uses expressions very much stronger than the meaning he really wishes to convey; as when he speaks of the "*everlasting* hills" or "the *boundless* ocean."

The hills are not really everlasting, but they are everlasting as compared with the structures of man. The ocean *has* bounds, but they are enormously wide. In the East this mode of speech is much more common than with us. An Arab chief will tell you there is nothing in his tent so much as worthy for you to set your foot on; but he would be very much astonished if you took him at his word. The oriental for some slight offence will declare that you and all your ancestors and all your descendants are the basest of mankind; and the next moment, on receiving a few piastres, be quite friendly with you, and tell you, you are the most illustrious son of an illustrious sire. The language deceives no one. It is understood to be mere hyperbole, and is common to all oriental nations. It frequently occurs in the Scriptures, *e.g.* when Christ says, "If any man come to Me, and *hate* not his father, and mother, and wife, and children, . . . and his own life also, he cannot be My disciple" (Luke xiv. 26), of course He does not mean that a disciple must literally hate his father and mother, but that he must not put *them* before *Him;* he must be willing even to forsake them for His sake. As he puts it in Matthew (x. 37), "He that loveth father or mother *more than Me* is not worthy of Me; and he that loveth son or daughter more than Me is not worthy of Me." So when Christ says, "Whosoever shall smite thee on the right cheek turn to him the other also," He does not mean the injunction to be literally obeyed. It is only a hyperbolical way of enjoining meekness and non-resistance. In like manner the passage which has so perplexed some readers, "It is easier for a camel to go through the eye of a needle than for a rich man to enter into the kingdom of God," would cause no difficulty to an oriental mind. Christ's hearers would at once understand, that He only meant it was exceedingly hard for a rich man to enter the kingdom. In the Old Testament, hyperbolical language is still more frequent than in the New. We give a few instances: "They were swifter than eagles, they were stronger than lions" (2 Sam. i. 23). "Then did I beat them small as the dust before the wind" (Psa. xviii. 42). "Rivers of water run down mine eyes because they keep not Thy law" (Psa. cxix. 136). "Their widows are increased to Me above the sand of the sea" (Jer. xv. 8).

8. **Parallelism.**—This is another common feature of oriental literature. It is especially distinctive of Eastern poetry, but is sometimes found in prose. Western poetry usually takes the form either of rhyme or blank verse. In the former case, the *sound* at the end of one line is made to correspond with the *sound* at the end of another. In the latter, the *number of the syllables* and the *fall of the accents* is made to correspond. Now, in Eastern poetry there is no attempt to make the final sounds correspond, and very little attention is paid to the measuring of syllables and accents; but the *thought* of one line is made to correspond with the *thought* of another, or several others. The lines run *parallel* in *thought*. There is no balance of sounds or accents, but a balance of ideas. This parallelism will be best exhibited in examples. Take the second Psalm. In what is called the "parallel" Bible you will find the first verse arranged thus—

> "Why do the heathen rage,
> And the people imagine a vain thing?"

Here the word "people" in the second line balances the "heathen" in the first; the "imagining a vain thing" in the second, the "raging" of the first. In this verse it is the same thought differently expressed in the two lines, and so it is all through this Psalm.

> { "The kings of the earth—set themselves;
> { Their rulers—take counsel together
>
> { Against the Lord
> { And against His Anointed (saying)

> Let us break—their bands asunder,
> And cast away—their cords from us.
>
> He that sitteth in the heavens—shall laugh ;
> The Lord—shall have them in derision," etc.

But in other cases the thought in the two lines is wholly different. Sometimes the second line expresses a *contrast* to the first:—

> "The Lord knoweth—the way of the righteous,
> But the way of the ungodly—shall perish;"

sometimes a *cause* or *consequence* of the first:—

> 'Depart from me all ye workers of iniquity,
> *For* the Lord hath heard the voice of my weeping."
>
> "Through thy precepts I get understanding,
> *Therefore* I hate every false way."

In the above examples we have the lines arranged in couplets; but they are sometimes found in triplets; as, for example, in the first Psalm:—

> "Blessed is the man
> That walketh not—in the counsel of the ungodly,
> Nor standeth—in the way of sinners,
> Nor sitteth—in the seat of the scornful."

But in all cases there is a balance of the sentences, a certain correspondence of the thought which is technically called "parallelism." The Book of Job, with the exception of the first two and the last chapters, the Psalms, the Proverbs, the Song of Solomon, and in general all the poetical books, are written in this style. It predominates in the prophetical books, and is found occasionally even in ordinary prose writing when the author rises to a height of impassioned feeling, as, for example, in 2 Cor. iv. 8–10.

> "We are troubled on every side—yet not distressed;
> We are perplexed—but not in despair;
>
> Persecuted—but not forsaken;
> Cast down—but not destroyed;

> Always bearing about in the body—the dying of the Lord Jesus;
> That the life also of Jesus—might be made manifest in our body."

Of course it appears in those poems which are sometimes introduced in the middle of historical books, as in the Patriarch's blessing (Gen. xlix.); the Song of Moses (Exod., xv.); the Song of Deborah (Jud. v.); the Song of "the Bow" (2 Sam. i. 19-27). One great advantage resulting from this form of Hebrew poetry is that it suffers far less by translation than if it had been of the nature of rhyme or blank verse. In process of translation rhyme and metre disappear. No doubt a version may be manufactured in the new language which shall have rhymes and metres; but then the accuracy of the translation has to be sacrificed in order to secure it. Again and again the word which would most exactly represent the original cannot be used, because it will not rhyme, or has not the accent which the metre requires; so another which is not so correct a translation has to be employed instead. Take the best metrical versions of the ancient classic poets who wrote in a rhythmical metre (*e.g.* Pope's Homer, or Dryden's Virgil), or take the recent English translations of the lyrical poems of Goethe and Heine written in rhyme, and you will see how much the sense has been altered in order to procure the right rhyme and rhythm, and how much of the beauty and force of the original is lost. But since in Scripture the poetry of the original consists not in rhyme and metre, but in the balance, the parallelism of the thought, a faithful translation always preserves this without any sacrifice.

9. These characteristics of language and style, even if we leave out of account the momentous truths revealed, make **the Bible a Unique Book**. There is none like it in any language. It combines the richness and glow of oriental literature, with the terseness and dramatic power of occidental; and displays a candour and impartiality, a simplicity and dignity to which no parallel can be found

in the histories either of the East or the West; while under all and through all the voice of the Eternal is heard, and the reader is made to feel the quite infinite difference between good and evil, between the man that serveth the Lord and the man that serveth him not. Hence it is that this book is fitted to be alike the guide of childhood and the comfort of old age, the Sunday school text-book, and the treasury whence the devout philosopher brings forth things new and old. "I know," says Professor Huxley, "that some of the pleasantest recollections of my childhood are connected with the voluntary study of an ancient Bible. There were splendid pictures in it, to be sure; but I recollect little or nothing about them save a picture of the high priest in his vestments. What comes vividly back on my mind are remembrances of my delight in the histories of Joseph and David; and of my keen appreciation of the chivalrous kindness of Abraham in his dealings with Lot. Like a sudden flash there returns upon me my utter scorn of the pettifogging meanness of Jacob, and my sympathetic grief over the heart-breaking lamentation of the cheated Esau—'Hast thou not a blessing for me also, O my father?' And I see as in a cloud the grand phantasmagoria of the Book of Revelation" (*Contemporary Review*, Dec. 1870). "Read to me," said Sir Walter Scott in his last hours, to his son-in-law. "What book shall I read to you?" said Lockhart. "Can you ask me?" Scott replied. "There is but *one*. Read me a chapter from the Gospel of John." Sir William Jones, the great oriental scholar, who was one of the first to make Europe acquainted with the riches of Persian and Arabian literature, says: "Theological inquiries form no part of my present subject; but I cannot refrain from adding, that the collection of tracts which we call from their excellence the Scriptures, contain (independently of a Divine origin) more true sublimity, more exquisite beauty, purer morality, more important history, and finer strains, both of poetry and eloquence, than could be collected within the same compass, from all other books that were ever composed in any age or in any idiom."

FOR REFERENCE AND FURTHER STUDY.

"Bible Words and Phrases." By Charles Michie. Macniven and Wallace.

"The Superhuman Origin of the Bible." By Prof. Henry Rogers. Hodder and Stoughton.

"The Four Gospels: with Dissertations and Notes." By Prof. George Campbell.

Chautauqua Text Books, No. 8: "What Noted Men Think of the Bible." No. 31: "What Noted Men Think of Christ." No. 1: "Biblical Exploration: A Condensed Manual on How to Study the Bible." No. 19: "The Book of Books." 10c. each.

CHAPTER IV.

ON THE STUDY OF SCRIPTURE WITH SPECIAL REFERENCE TO SUNDAY SCHOOL INSTRUCTION, AND SOME REMARKS ON SCRIPTURE DIFFICULTIES.

THE subject of this chapter is a very wide one. Our general object is to put the teacher into such a way of studying his Bible, that he may be able to use it to the best advantage as the handbook of class instruction. If he would so use it, he must know a great deal more about it than he intends to communicate to his scholars. As with any single portion which may form the lesson for the day, the teacher who has thoroughly prepared his lesson will always have in his head many more ideas about the passage than he purposes to utter with his lips; so with regard to the book as a whole, if he would be an efficient teacher, his own researches into its construction and contents must go much beyond what is unfolded in the course of his instruction. What he speaks will be a *selection* from what he knows. The wider knowledge (whether of the particular lesson or the whole book) will enable him to select what is most appropriate to the understanding and circumstances of his class, to present what he does present in a more forcible and interesting way, to avoid errors and possible sources of misunderstanding, and will beside give him a sense of power and mastery over the subject which the scholars will *feel*, though they may be ignorant of its cause.

In this little book we can only lay down a few broad principles, give a few general directions, to aid the teacher in his study of Scripture; and perhaps he will not at once perceive the bearing even of some of these on his special work. But we trust that enlarged experience will show him the value of them, and that the first, at any rate, will commend itself to his understanding.

1. **The Bible a Book of Human Life.**—Let him study the Bible as a book that is concerned throughout with living men and women, with a nature like his own. In this respect it differs from the sacred books of most other religions. It is not like the Zend-Avesta, or the maxims of Confucius, or that exceedingly dull and uninteresting book, the Koran of Mahomet. It is not a code of laws, or a directory of the conscience, or a system of theology. True, it contains the highest law; it affords valuable direction to the conscience; and all Christian theology is based on it. But it is not in itself a code, or a directory, or a system, still less a mere string of texts. To look at it in that way, to study it in that way, is fatal to success as a Sunday school teacher. It is a BOOK OF LIFE in every sense of the words. It is the record of God's Spirit working in the hearts of men, and drawing them to Himself. Two-thirds of it is history, and of the remaining third by far the largest portion is connected most closely with the lives of the men who wrote it, and can only be rightly understood when those lives are understood. Take the Psalms. No doubt they are inspired; the working of God's Spirit is nowhere more evident than in these sublime productions; but all through we hear the passionate beating of a human heart—a heart like our own, a heart that groans in distress and rejoices in deliverance, that bleeds under the cruel treachery of a false friend, and resents the calumnies of lying enemies,—a heart that has its alternations of feeling like ours, now depressed and despondent, now elate with joy and gratitude. Take the Prophets.

They were not hermits dwelling in cells or caves apart from their kind, but men who took an active part in the most stirring events of their day. If we read aright the prophecies of Isaiah, Jeremiah, etc., we shall see these servants of the Lord maintaining a vigorous conflict with the powers of evil in various forms, contending against time-serving priests and intriguing politicians, inveighing against the various social evils which were dragging the people downwards towards lower and lower depths of corruption, rebuking the increase of luxurious living, the oppression of the poor by the rich, the extravagance of the fine ladies of Jerusalem in dress, the dissoluteness and drunkenness of the men; and anon throwing themselves into the struggle of political parties, and earnestly warning the king against State alliances that must ultimately lead to the downfall of the nation. Or take once more the Epistles of Paul. They introduce us at once into the atmosphere of active Church life. We have already gained incidentally a glimpse into the affairs of the Church at Corinth (in our first chapter) with its sectarian tendencies, its petty cliques, its grave scandals, its excitement over some of the problems of social life, and its somewhat disorderly assemblies. We seem to see Paul's messengers passing to and fro with the letters, his anxiety in awaiting the result, the actual administration of discipline on the most glaring offender, and Paul's subsequent joy at the general obedience of the Church, and his tender care lest severity carried too far should crush into despair the excluded member. In the Epistle to the Galatians we see the growth of what we should call Ritualism, and the arguments which Paul employed against it, arguments which are for the most part equally applicable in the present day. We have in the second chapter a graphic description of the contention between the Judaizing party and the party of Christian liberty, and all through the Epistle little personal touches which place Paul's connection with the Church in the most vivid light. In the

Epistle to the Philippians we have the picture of a church that gave its founder almost unmingled satisfaction, though even there the quarrel between two of the female members calls for a word of gentle admonition (Phil. iv. 2, 3). But the letter is brimming over with affection and gratitude, which was as heartily returned on the part of the Church; and this Epistle, read in connection with the story of the founding of the Church (Acts xvi.), becomes as interesting and as full of life as any page that could be taken from our modern missionary records. Even the little Epistle to Philemon, what a lesson it makes for the Sunday school teacher that knows how to handle it! What a touching story it unfolds of the good Christian master and the ungrateful slave, stealing his master's goods and running away to Rome, there meeting with Paul and by him converted, helping the apostle for a while, and then sent back to his master (who was himself one of Paul's converts) with this letter of Paul's, pleading for forgiveness in his name.

Now it is true that Sunday school lessons from the Psalms, Prophets, and Epistles, are not often taken except with senior classes; but they might be made interesting even to junior classes, if the teacher would only take pains to get at the *life* that is in them. It is to be feared that even in the narrative lessons this is often imperfectly realized and inadequately brought out. Certainly the scholars will not realize it without the teacher's aid. They have a general impression that the Bible came down from God; they have no notion that it grew up out of the lives of men. The places and persons of Scripture are for them invested with an air of unreality. The young woman who was astonished at hearing that there was even now a *real* country called Egypt, who had "always thought it was only a place in the Bible," is a type of the great mass of our scholars. It is the teachers' business to disabuse their minds of this impression by making the incidents and scenes and personages of Scripture stand before their eyes as in real life, and by showing them how *all* the language of Scripture came from, and was addressed to, human beings, living as men, women, and children do to-day. But of course the teacher will not be able to do this unless he has first realized it for himself. He must exert his imagination; he must put himself in the place of the persons of whom he speaks; he must *be* (for the time) the blind Bartimæus, the sinking Peter, the shipwrecked Paul, the runaway Onesimus. But mere exertion of the imagination will not suffice. He must *find* the life before he pictures it; and to find the life, he must look for it, keep his eye open for every little passing word (like those verses, Phil. iv. 2, 3) that discloses the life, and he must gather up from all sources such information as will enable him to follow the thread of Scripture history, to understand incidental allusions, and to transfer himself in thought to the scene to which his lesson refers. Of these studies we will speak presently. But let the teacher understand, that till he can present the lesson to his scholars as full of life, he has not thoroughly prepared it. Children will listen to anything that tells of life. They will not listen to dry doctrine or moral preachment. It is well if the teacher illustrate the teaching of Scripture with incidents from real life outside it; but it is better if he can make his scholars feel that the Bible itself is full of life from beginning to end.

2. **Progress of Divine Revelation.**—Another thing which the teacher must keep in view in his study of the Scriptures is the Progress of Divine Revelation traceable therein. This point is closely connected with the last, and, like it, has been often overlooked. The Bible is the record of God's successive revelations to His chosen people, and through them to mankind. Now the human race has its childhood, and each nation has its childhood, just as every individual person has his childhood. The Bible takes the Hebrew nation in its childhood, and shows us how God

trained them in righteousness, and educated them in the knowledge of Himself. If we have to educate a child, we do not attempt to teach it everything at once. We teach it a few simple things first, and we teach those in a very simple way. We are content that it should have rough general notions on many subjects, and should remain quite ignorant of others until it is older. So with its moral training; we do not attempt to instil grand notions of complete self-sacrifice and heroic devotion, nor discuss with it any of the difficult moral problems that arise out of the complicated relations of human life. We teach it a few simple virtues, and endeavour to cure it of its most open faults. We teach it largely by pictures, fables, and stories; and lead it on by degrees. Now the Bible, as we have said, tells us about the childhood of the Jewish nation—takes us, in fact, to its very birth. The patriarch Jacob was the beginning, the progenitor of all the Jews. And he and his father Isaac and his grandfather Abraham were in many respects like children; very simple-minded, and, as we should now say, wholly uneducated men; shepherds who had led their flocks across the Jordan from the countries to the East, where nature-worship and idolatry prevailed. Their notions of God were very crude; their worship exceedingly simple. Books they had none—for they knew nothing of reading or writing, and their minds were unformed, unaccustomed to thought, like a child's. And when Moses led the Israelites out of Egypt they were still children, in some respects worse than children; for they had been in slavery for several generations, and hard servitude always hardens, coarsens, and brutalizes a people. Now, manifestly in the very nature of things, it was impossible that God should teach either the patriarch or this horde of escaped slaves what he has taught us in Jesus Christ, nor even what he taught the Jews in their later history by the prophets. He could neither teach them the same things nor teach them in the same way. They would not have been able to understand it. They had to be broken of their worst faults, their rude and savage nature controlled, and their minds instructed in a rudimentary knowledge of God and his law. This was done partly by express commandments, partly by the institution of sacrifice and the priestly ritual. That ritual, with its white-robed priests, its bleeding victims, its washings and purifications, has been called not inaptly, "the Jews' Picture Book." God was teaching them by these pictures, the beauty of holiness, the horribleness of sin, the certainty that sin entails suffering, the need of vicarious sacrifice, the duty of serving God with their best, and the necessity of keeping themselves pure, and avoiding contamination by contact with heathen defilement, if they would serve Him acceptably. Along with this, and indeed prior to this, they were taught to look upon God as the Eternal Self-existent One (Jehovah, I AM, or rather He who *is*, the One that ever is), righteous and merciful, who had singled them out to be His people, and who would punish all idolatry and apostasy from him. The law of Moses (even if we were to limit that expression to the ten commandments) shows a wonderful knowledge of human nature; and an exalted morality which can only be attributed to a Divine Author; but God did not intend it as a final declaration of His will; but as something adapted to the condition of the people at that time—the best and highest revelation they were then capable of receiving, but by no means complete or absolute. This, Christ makes very plain by his own teaching. Referring to the easy divorcement of wives permitted by the Mosaic law, he says, "Moses, because of the hardness of your hearts, suffered you to put away your wives; but from the beginning it was not so"—*i.e.* in the Divine intention, when man and woman were first created, the one was to be for the other throughout life; but (after the fall of man) this Divine intention could only be realized by degrees. On the same principle the permission of polygamy by the

Mosaic law is to be explained. Again, in the Sermon on the Mount, he says, quoting from the Book of Exodus, "Ye have heard that it hath been said, 'An eye for an eye and a tooth for a tooth,' but *I* say unto you that ye resist not evil." The people in their rough, half-barbarous state, needed these stern laws; but Christ, when they were ready for it, unfolded a higher and a milder one. (Compare similar instances in the same Sermon on the Mount.)

Again, with regard *to the mode of worshipping and serving God*, the progress of Divine revelation may be distinctly traced. An outward ritual, a consecrated temple and priesthood, sacrifices and oblations were needed to enable the people in the earlier stages of their development to realize that God was really present amongst them, that they were to serve Him with the best they had, that all sin was a grievous offence to Him, and that it necessarily entailed suffering on the innocent as well as on the guilty. Not till the full light of the Christian revelation dawned, and Christ had appeared to put away sin by the sacrifice of himself, was this ritual done away; but we observe how, throughout the intervening period, God was teaching the people more and more plainly, that this ritual was merely *representative*, that *spiritual* sacrifice was what He really required. The Psalmist says, "Thou desirest not sacrifice, else would I give it; Thou delightest not in burnt offering. The sacrifices of God are a broken spirit; a broken and a contrite heart, O God, Thou wilt not despise." And again, "Sacrifice and burnt offering Thou didst not desire; . . . burnt offering and sin offering hast Thou not required. Then said I, Lo, I come: in the volume of the book it is written of me, *to do Thy will*, O my God; yea, Thy law is within my heart." (See also similar teaching in the fiftieth Psalm.) But the people were slow to accept this spiritual teaching. It was so much easier to bring the outward sacrifice of the ox or the lamb, than the inward sacrifice of the heart. They clung to the notion that if they only observed the external ritual they could live pretty much as they liked. So we find the prophets earnestly contending against this notion, and persistently striving to instil higher ideas of what the law of God really required. Thus Isaiah, speaking in the name of the Lord, pours contempt upon the sacrifices, feasts, and fasts that were observed without the accompaniment of a renewed heart and life. "To what purpose is the multitude of your sacrifices unto me? saith the Lord. I am full of the burnt offerings of rams, and the fat of fed beasts. . . . Bring no more vain oblations. . . . Your hands are full of blood. Wash you, make you clean; put away the evil of your doings from before Mine eyes; cease to do evil; learn to do well; seek judgment, relieve the oppressed, judge the fatherless; plead for the widow. Come *now*, and let us reason together, saith the Lord: though your sins be as scarlet, they shall be as white as snow; though they be red like crimson, they shall be as wool" (Isa. i. 11–18). In like manner, Micah (vi. 6–8): "Wherewith shall I come before the Lord, and bow myself before the most high God? Shall I come before Him with burnt offerings, with calves of a year old? Will the Lord be pleased with thousands of rams, or with ten thousands of rivers of oil? Shall I give my firstborn for my transgression, the fruit of my body for the sin of my soul? He hath showed thee, O man, what is good; and what doth the Lord require of thee, but to do justly, and to love mercy, and to walk humbly with thy God?" Many similar passages might be quoted from the prophets, showing how, in the progress of Divine revelation, the teaching became more spiritual; less importance was attached to the outward rites, and more to the inward dispositions and acts of which they were symbolic. One mark of this progress is the diminishing importance of the priest, the growing importance of the prophet. In the earlier history of the Israelites, the priests are the most prominent representatives of the Lord;

in the later, the prophets. The priests were only the authorized performers of the external acts of worship, and their duties were fixed once for all. The prophets were inspired to teach God's will in matters of the heart and life. They got their message fresh from Him, a message suited to the people's need in every age. They revealed more and more plainly the character of God, and his purposes concerning his people. The function of the priests was ceremonial, the function of the prophets spiritual; and so in the progressive education of the people the office of the priest dwindled in significance, and the prophets became the highest and truest representatives of God.

This brings us to notice one more feature in the progress of Divine revelation, which is indeed the most important, and largely the cause of the others: we mean *the gradual unfolding of God's own nature and character.* Even in the earlier stages of revelation He revealed himself to the Jews as He had done to no other people. His character as unfolded to His servant Moses at the very beginning of their history is sublime in its perfect purity and awful righteousness, tempered with mercy for those who would bow to Him and keep His commandments. It stands immeasurably above the conception of Deity formed by other nations of antiquity. It was an advance upon the idea the patriarchs had of Him.* But the people in those early times were not capable of appreciating all the beauty and tenderness of the Divine character, nor able to apprehend the purely spiritual nature of the Divine Being. They could only learn this by degrees. In the earlier books, God permitted His servants to speak of Him somewhat after the fashion of a man, with emotions and senti-

* From the narrative, Gen. xxviii. 10-22, it would appear that Jacob had not yet learned that his father's God was present in every place (ver. 16); and that he thought of Him as one God out of many, whom he *might choose* for his own (vers. 20, 21); moreover, as a God whom he might put to the test, and with whom he might conclude a sort of bargain (vers. 20, 22).

ments akin to those of human nature, and even with bodily attributes. In the later books more spiritual ideas are presented, but His worship is still to some extent localized. He is thought of as being more present, or at least more favourable to the worshippers, in one place than another. It needed a gradual education to prepare the minds of the people for Christ's teaching concerning God: "Woman, believe Me, the hour cometh, when ye shall neither in this mountain, nor at Jerusalem, worship the Father. The hour cometh, and now is, when the true worshippers shall worship the Father in spirit and in truth: for the Father seeketh such to worship Him. *God is Spirit*, and they that worship Him must worship Him in spirit and in truth." Again, in the Pentateuch God is presented chiefly in the light of a *Judge*, not, indeed, an unmerciful Judge, but still strict to mark iniquity, chiefly concerned to punish transgression and reward obedience. Later on, the idea of Judge is merged in the wider one of Sovereign, Ruler and Sustainer of all things. Then we find in the later prophets the idea of God as a *Father* slowly emerging. At first simply by way of *comparison*: "*Like as* a father pitieth his children, so the Lord pitieth them that fear Him" (Psa. ciii. 13). Then more directly, but still rather as a Father to the *nation* than the individual: "I am a Father to Israel, and Ephraim is My firstborn" (Jer. xxxi. 9); "Doubtless Thou art our Father" (Isa. lxiii. 16). At last, in the New Testament of the well-beloved Son, the full-orbed truth shines out: "The one God and Father of all," "not of the Jews only, but of the Gentiles," for "we are all His offspring." Throughout Christ's discourses it is the most frequent name for God; and all over the pages of the Gospels and Epistles, the words, "Our Father," "Your Father," "The Father," sparkle out thick as the stars in heaven. We have fastened on the *name* as bringing the fact most clearly to light. But it is not only a new name given to God, but an enlarged conception of His nature which sums up in itself the ideas of Judge, Ruler, and Sustainer, while it includes much more beside, the "righteous Father."

Did the limits of this work permit, we should be glad to trace the progress of Divine revelation as manifested in other aspects, particularly the gradual development of the doctrine of the Future Life; but we must be content to have indicated its existence and general course. We commend the further study of it to the Sunday school teacher, both as interesting and instructive in itself, and as being the key to many of the Scripture difficulties which he will meet with in preparation for his class.

3. **Bible History.**—To this end, if for no other reason, the teacher must *study his Bible historically;* and he will constantly find himself at a loss in teaching if he has not done so. He need not be prepared to give the exact date of every event in Scripture history. The exact chronology of some parts of the Bible is involved in considerable difficulties.* It will be enough for him to use the dates at the head of the columns of the newer reference Bibles as sufficiently accurate for his purpose. But he should have a general outline of Scripture history clearly fixed in his mind; and should know at what points of the history the non-historical books (such as the prophets) fit in. Some information on the latter subject has already been given in the chapter on the Canon. We now subjoin a brief compendium, "a bird's eye view" of Jewish history which the student should master thoroughly.

The patriarchs from whom the Jewish race descended came originally from the country east of the Euphrates, and after many wanderings in the land of Canaan, migrated to Egypt, where their descendants were enslaved by the kings of that country. Moses led them out about fifteen hundred years before Christ; and after forty years' wandering in the wilderness, his successor, Joshua, brought them into the promised land. For some four hundred years

---

* See Appendix, Note C.

they struggled with the inhabitants of that country. During this period there was no central government; but a succession of "Judges," or local chieftains, arising sometimes in one tribe, sometimes in another, obtained a temporary leadership. The first king, Saul, about 1100 B.C. subjugated many of the hostile clans, and under his successors, David and Solomon, the whole of Palestine was won for the Jewish crown, and also a large extent of territory east of the Jordan, reaching almost to the Euphrates. In the reign of Rehoboam, the ten northern tribes revolted, and formed the kingdom of Israel; the two southern tribes, Judah and Benjamin, remained united, and formed the kingdom of Judah. There were thus two lines of kings reigning at the same time. The two kingdoms were often at war with each other, and called in the surrounding nations to help them. The northern kingdom was larger but weaker than the southern. The kings' reigns were shorter, being frequently cut short by violence, and the throne transferred from one family to another. The kings were all more or less idolatrous, and about the year 720 B.C. the punishment often foretold came upon them from the Lord. They were conquered by the Assyrians, and a large number of them carried captive, leaving the southern portion of their territory (around Samaria) quite bare, so that it was afterwards repeopled by heathen. The reigns of the kings of Judah were longer and more peaceful. The throne continued in the line of David's descendants. Some of them made vigorous efforts to suppress idolatry, and they continued to reign for a hundred and thirty-five years after the northern kingdom had perished. But since they, too, proved in the end unfaithful, they brought upon themselves Divine judgment. The Babylonians, who had in the mean time conquered the Assyrians, invaded Judah, and in three successive inroads almost depopulated the land, though a remnant of the poorer sort of Jews were left behind (486 B.C.). After seventy years the Babylonians (or Chaldees) were themselves conquered by Cyrus the Persian, and this monarch gave permission to the Jewish exiles to return to their native land. A goodly number did so under the leadership of a prince named Zerubbabel, and bestirred themselves on their arrival to repeople the waste cities and rebuild the temple. But the work went on slowly till the arrival of Ezra, and twelve years later, of Nehemiah (444 B.C.). By Zerubbabel the temple, and by Nehemiah the walls of Jerusalem were rebuilt. By their united efforts the people were to a large extent purified from heathen alliances; the law of the Lord, particularly as regards the Sabbath, was enforced; and the priestly service re-instituted. Here the Old Testament history breaks off, about four hundred years before Christ. At this time Palestine was subject to Persia. But Persia with all her dominions was conquered by Alexander the Great, and in this way the Greek language and Greek influence spread over the Jewish colonies and penetrated the Holy Land itself. When the empire of Alexander was broken up, Syria and Egypt struggled for the possession of Palestine during a period of a hundred and forty years, in the course of which the Jews, led on by their high priests, achieved for a time their independence. When at last Rome became mistress of the world, Julius Cæsar took away the government from the high priests and made Herod the Great (an Idumean or Edomite) king of the whole country. Subsequently Judæa and Samaria became part of the Roman province of Syria, and were governed by a Roman procurator resident at Cæsarea, while Galilee was a little monarchy (or tetrarchy) owing allegiance to the Roman emperor, but governed independently by Herod Antipas, son of Herod the Great. This was the state of things during the lifetime of our Lord. After his death Herod Agrippa (a grandson of Herod the Great) was allowed to reign for a short time over the whole of Palestine (Acts xii.). But afterwards Judæa and Samaria were again placed under procurators. In A.D. 66 the Jews, exasperated at their avarice, revolted against the Romans, and drove them out of the Holy Land altogether But the Roman emperors Vespasian and Titus took summary vengeance, ravaged the north of Palestine, and in A.D. 70 utterly destroyed Jerusalem, and blotted the Jews (as a nation) out of existence.

4. The **Geography** of Palestine and the neighbouring countries should be studied along with the history; but for this subject we must refer the reader to some of the Sunday school manuals, where he can study it with the aid of maps.

Similarly with regard to the **Natural History** of the Bible, the distinguishing features of the **Jewish Sects**, and the **Manners and Customs** of the people. A knowledge of the last in particular is absolutely necessary to the understanding of almost every portion of the Bible. Without it the Sunday school teacher will be liable to fall into even ludicrous mistakes in his exposition of the lesson, and will be unable to give it that vivid colouring which will interest the children. One little book will supply him with abundant information on these and many other Biblical topics; and whatever other book he lacks, he should procure a copy of the "Aids to Bible Students," printed by Eyre and Spottiswoode, and published by the Society for the Promotion of Christian Knowledge, in a variety of types and binding, costing from one shilling upwards It is not to be confounded with the "Helps to the Study of the Bible," a similar but somewhat inferior work. The latter is bound up with the Oxford Bible, the former (which we recommend) with the Sunday School Teachers' "Variorum" Bible.

5. As regards a **Plan for the Study of Scripture**, we would observe that the *worst* plan of all is to read the Bible straight through from Genesis to Revelation. This may be done after the separate portions of the book have been thoroughly studied on another plan; but **for many**

reasons it is not the best to start with. It is best to take one book at a time, and fairly master its contents. Many things not noticed at a first reading will attract attention at a second or a third, and many points imperfectly understood at first will become clear on reperusal. Moreover, a better idea of the general aim and scope of the book will be obtained in this way, especially if, after studying it in sections, the student can find time to sit down and read through the whole at one sitting. This last remark applies most emphatically to the Prophecies and Epistles. If the student asks, "Where, then, shall I begin?" we would reply with the Gospels. There would, indeed, be some advantage in studying the Old Testament first; but life is short; the revelation made in the person of Jesus Christ is of supreme importance, and, on the whole, we would recommend the student to begin with it. The study of the Gospels simultaneously in parallel passages present too many difficulties for the beginner. Let him be content to take each separately, and, when he has become thoroughly familiar with the life, character, and teaching of Christ as there exhibited, let him go on to the Book of Acts, and learn how "the words of this life" took hold upon the world. Let him, then, take up the Epistles of Paul, and, before reading each, let him turn back to the Acts, and find out all he can about the people to whom it was written and Paul's connection with them. Then let him study the other Epistles. The Epistle to the Hebrews will make him eager to commence the study of the Old Testament, to which he may now turn. He has gained a clear idea of the great end to which God had been working for ages and generations, and may profitably trace the successive steps by which the Divine plan was accomplished. He may read straight on in the order of our Bibles till he comes to the end of the Second Book of Kings. Then let him study the writings of those prophets who lived in the times of the kings in the following order:

Jonah, Joel, Amos, Hosea, Obadiah, Isaiah (i.–xxxix.), Micah, Jeremiah, Lamentations, Zephaniah, Nahum, Habbakkuk. He will find here frequent references to the history in the Kings, and the parallel account in the Chronicles, which cover the same period, though written later. He should read this book before passing on to the prophets who wrote in the time of the exile: Isaiah (xl.–lxvi.), Ezekiel, and Daniel. Then the Book of Esther, the account of the return from exile in Ezra and Nehemiah, and, last, the prophets who lived after the return—Haggai, Zechariah, and Malachi. It is assumed that the Book of Psalms will be read as a book of devotion simultaneously with this more systematic study of Scripture; and the books not yet mentioned may be taken up after it is concluded, viz. Job, Song of Solomon, Ecclesiastes, Proverbs, and Revelation, all of which are comparatively independent of the history, and may be equally well understood without reference to it, while certain difficulties of interpretation make them fitter objects for later study. If time can be spared both for a morning and an evening reading, the study of the two Testaments, according to the above plan, may be carried forward together with great advantage.

6. A few hints on the **Preparation of the Lesson**, though scarcely falling within the scope of this book, may not be unacceptable. The teacher will probably follow the International series. If left to select his own lesson, we would advise him in general to choose some *narrative*, especially if his scholars are young and his own experience of teaching slight. Doctrinal and topical lessons are better suited for old classes, and require more judgment and ability to make them interesting. We presume that the teacher is furnished with some external aid, such as is now so abundantly supplied for the "lesson for the day" in the *Sunday School Chronicle* and similar publications. But we would strongly urge him, before looking at it, to

study the passage, with prayer for Divine assistance, *by himself*. If he understands the general drift of it, let him not even open a commentary or book of reference, but ask himself first, "Now, what does this passage teach *me?* What feature of Christ's character or God's government does it bring out? What sin does it warn against, or what virtue does it inculcate, or what duty does it set before me?" If he will patiently read and think, some one point will probably emerge and fasten his attention. He will feel, "Now, this is *the* truth that comes out in the passage, and I must make the children see it as I see it, and feel it as I feel it." If the teacher always leans on the crutches of commentary and lesson outline to give him his first idea, his mind will grow lame and impotent. He will best cultivate its powers by using them first independently, to draw out of Holy Writ the meaning God has put there; and he will put the point of the lesson with much greater freshness and vigour to his children, if it is something which he has thought out for himself and not picked up out of a book. Then let him set to work to see that he understands not only the general drift, but every portion of the lesson. Are there any *words* in the lesson that will need explaining to the children? Are there any *places* whose situation must be described to them? Are these places mentioned elsewhere in Holy Writ? Have there been events connected with them (either in the Bible or out of it) which might be briefly referred to in a way to interest the children or might be drawn from them by questions? Similarly with regard to *persons* mentioned in the narrative. Who are they? What are their antecedents? How came they to be there? This will most likely lead him to study the *connection* in which the passage stands, a matter which should always receive attention. Let him further note whether there are any allusions to *oriental modes* of life which the children will not understand without explanation. In gathering this information, the teacher will be glad to consult his *Sunday School Chronicle* and other books of reference, and in so doing may get some further suggestions. Having now amassed his material, let him draw out the plan of his lesson. Various lesson-plans are given in teachers' manuals. The plan should be varied frequently. The most natural and serviceable for common use is as follows:—

(i.) Introduction, which may take the form of the historical connection between the present and the last lesson, or of some question or anecdote leading up to and awakening interest in the subject of the day.

(ii.) Reading of the passage, with needful explanations, and illustration of subordinate points.

(iii.) Bringing out the main point of the lesson, if possible, from the scholars themselves by means of questions.

(iv.) Enforcement of the same by illustration and appeal.

(v.) Questioning on what has been taught.

The teacher should remember, when seeking for illustrations, that the Bible itself is a repertory of moral and religious anecdote. The less-read portions of Scripture history, such as the Book of Judges, second Book of Kings, the Books of Esther and Nehemiah, are full of striking life-pictures, which will be new to the scholars, and from which illustrations may be drawn for a great variety of subjects. If the lesson for the day be not itself a portion of Scripture narrative, but on some special topic or doctrine, it is all the more desirable that the illustration should be drawn from the sacred page itself. It will be seen that we have taken for granted that there will be always some main point, some central truth which the teacher means to make *the* lesson of the day, and on which he will concentrate his powers. Occasionally there will be two, or even three, which seem equally important; but, as a rule, the most effective teaching is that which aims at producing one solid impression, driving one truth home at each lesson. This method has further the advantage of giving graphic variety to the teaching as a whole, whereas, if the teacher allows himself to wander over a number of points, morals, and maxims at each lesson, some of these necessarily recurring again and again will leave on the class an impression that "Teacher's lessons are all alike. He is always saying the same thing." We have only to add, that when in a course of lessons a fresh book of scripture is commenced, the teacher should read the whole through himself, that he may see what is coming, observe what passages in the book are best adapted to enforce certain truths, and, having these in his mind, be on the look out for any illustrations that may present themselves in his general reading or daily life, and jot them down in his note-book or blank-leaved Bible. If he is teaching a fairly advanced class, he should at the first lesson tell them all he knows about the date and the author of the book, and give them some idea of its general scope and purpose.

7. **Scripture Difficulties.**—No wise teacher will *start* difficulties in his class, but he should be prepared to solve them when presented by his scholars. Moreover, even should his scholars not bring them up in class, the consciousness of them in his own mind (if he does not see his way through them) will hamper his freedom, and impair his pleasure and efficiency in teaching.

(i) Some minds find a difficulty in believing in miracles at all. The subject is too wide to be discussed in these pages. We can only refer the reader who desires to go into it to standard works on the subject, such as Canon Mozley's "Bampton Lecture," Trench's "Notes on the Miracles of our Lord" (Preliminary Essay), Bushnell's "Nature and the Supernatural," etc.

(ii.) There is sometimes *a difficulty in reconciling two statements of fact* in different parts of the sacred record; *e.g.* Matthew mentions the healing of *two* blind men as Christ was *leaving* Jericho; Mark mentions only one;

Luke mentions only one, and that one as being healed by Christ when he was *entering* the town. Now, upon this and all similar discrepancies of fact we would observe, first, that a perfectly complete knowledge of all the circumstances might enable us to harmonize the two accounts perfectly. We might, for instance, find that, though there were indeed two blind men, one of them, Bartimeus, was throughout the leader and spokesman; Mark, in reporting his case, reported all that seemed to him necessary; further, that the cure took place after Christ had been some time in the town, somewhere in the outskirts, when Christ was about to re-enter the town and pass through it on his way to some other place. If this were so it might be said to be " as he was *entering* Jericho " or "as he was *leaving* Jericho," according as the writer regarded the immediate direction of Christ's steps, or his purpose of immediately departing from the town. We do not say it *was* so (other explanations have been suggested), but it shows how a fuller knowledge might remove all difficulty. The records are only fragmentary: each writer gives the account from his own point of view; and this leads us to observe, secondly, that such apparent contradictions *almost invariably* occur whenever a number of thoroughly independent witnesses report an event that they have witnessed in common: one saw something that the other did not, or saw the same thing from a different point. Now, if we can have the witnesses before us and question them, we can generally unravel the difficulty and bring the accounts into perfect agreement. Where this cannot be done (as of course it cannot in the case of the evangelists) it would still be highly unreasonable to discard their concurrent testimony to the main facts as worthless because of some apparent contradictions in minor details. The present writer has in his possession four accounts of the assassination of the Russian Emperor Nicholas II., by the explosion of a bomb beneath his carriage in the streets of St. Petersburg on Sunday, March 13, 1881. They were transmitted direct from the spot, two of them by eye-witnesses. They contain more and graver discrepancies than those to be found among our evangelists concerning any event which they relate in common. Some of them were reconciled in subsequent reports, some of them remain unreconciled to this day. The four accounts were published in the daily papers, and we venture to say that not one person of the thousands who read them ever doubted for a moment that the Czar had been assassinated by the explosion of a bomb beneath his carriage on that memorable Sunday. Hence the Bible student, even when unable to reconcile these small differences in the record, may rest with unimpaired confidence in its veracity. These differences show that we have the testimony of really independent witnesses. Had there been absolute and perfect agreement in all details, it would have afforded some ground for the suspicion either that three of the evangelists had simply copied from the fourth; or that they had all agreed together to concoct the same story.

(iii.) It sometimes appears as though the *doctrine* of Scripture in one place disagreed with the *doctrine* in another. Where it is a passage from the Old Testament as compared with the New, it will generally be found that the latter really includes the former, enlarges and goes beyond it, as in the instances already given (§ 2) from Christ's Sermon on the Mount; that it is, in fact, an instance of the progress of Divine revelation. In other cases it will be discovered that the passages really refer to different things, though both are called by the same name. Thus, when Paul says a man is saved by faith without works, *he* means by faith, *loyal trust* in the Redeemer. When James says a man is *not* saved by faith without works, and that "faith without works is dead being alone," *he* means by faith mere *intellectual assent* to the truths of the gospel. Again, when Paul speaks of "works," he is thinking chiefly of the rites and formal service of the law. But James means by works the deeds of a holy life. The "works" of James will inevitably follow from the "faith" of Paul. They are the fruit and the sign of it; but faith as being the *root* is put forward by Paul as the means of salvation. So Paul's doctrine and James' doctrine are reconciled in the paradox, "A man is saved by faith without works, but, a man is not saved by *the* faith that is without works," because that is not true faith at all. Mistranslation is often the cause of apparent contradictions, as of some other kinds of Scripture difficulties. A good commentary will generally supply the needful correction.

(iv.) *The bad actions of good men in Scripture* constitute another common difficulty Some people seem to think that because certain men are in general terms described as righteous and approved of God, therefore everything that they did ought to be right. But this is a serious error. There is no ground for such a supposition. It would be most unnatural if it were so. Human nature in its *main features* continues the same in all ages ; and as there is a leaven of evil even in the best men now, so it was in the days of Scripture history. The fact that the evil is there plainly recorded shows how impartial the record is, and (as we have already pointed out) indicates Divine guidance in the composition of it. But perhaps it will be urged that some of the deeds of good men are so *very* bad; that David is called "the man after God's own heart," and yet he is guilty of murder, adultery, and horrible cruelty to his vanquished foes. Now, upon this we observe, first, that the men of that primitive and half-barbarous age must not be judged by the high standard of morality which Christ set up; secondly, that David is not called *the* man after God's own heart, but simply *a* man after God's own heart, *i.e.* in comparison with Saul, who proved utterly faithless and rebellious. It is never even implied that he was the man who most fully came up to the Divine ideal; on the contrary, his murder and adultery drew on him God's emphatic condemnation and most severe punishment; and "because he had been a man of blood" he was not allowed to build a temple to the Lord.

(v.) But it will still further be urged, perhaps, that *some evil things were done with Divine approval* and even by Divine command: such as the extermination of the Canaanites, the treacherous murder of Sisera, the slaughter of Saul's sons, etc. Now, we admit the difficulty, but remind the student, first, in general that we are not competent to sit in judgment on all the Divine actions; secondly, that this is peculiarly the case with reference to times and circumstances so remote from our own, and such vast problems as are involved in the condemnation of sinful nations and the setting up of a people through whom the whole world was to be benefited; thirdly, that if we find in the course of nature a whole population decimated or even swept away by pestilence and famine, including many comparatively innocent persons, it is *no greater difficulty* if, by direction of the Author of Nature, the entire population of some of the Canaanite cities was cut off by the sword of Israel; and then, fourthly, we are not always certain how far the prophets really understood the mind of God when they spoke of Him as commanding certain things. In many cases we know the Divine will was ascertained by the casting of lots or some similar process, and it is fairly open to question whether this was a legitimate way of seeking direction, whether the response elicited was really a declaration of the will of God. We cannot enlarge on these points, but commend them to the thoughtful consideration of the teacher who is troubled by this class of difficulties. We also ask him to bear in mind what we have said in a former section of this chapter about the progressive character of Divine revelation. That alone will remove the difficulty which he must feel in reading—

(vi.) *The Imprecatory Psalms:* such as Psa. cix. No doubt

the language here employed concerning the psalmist's enemies is vindictive to the last degree. Our mind and conscience, educated under the influence of the gospel, recoils from it. It does not help us, to be told that the psalmist's enemies were also the enemies of the Lord; for we could not use such language with reference to the wickedest man we ever knew. What we have to remember is, that the Psalm was written nearly three thousand years ago, by a member of that nation which God was gradually disciplining in holiness. He could not teach them everything at once. He taught them to love righteousness and hate iniquity. He trained them in the sterner virtues first. The tenderer sentiments were to be inculcated afterwards. It was reserved for His Son to teach how we were to love our enemies, do good to those that hate us, and pray for them that despitefully use us and persecute us. The ancient Jews were not ripe for that lesson. Even we do not find it an easy one. We do not find it easy to hate sin, yet pity and even love the sinner. To the mind of the psalmist the two would appear incompatible. In his vehement indignation against his enemies who broke the law of God and persecuted him because he was the servant of God, he found himself unable to separate between the sinner and his sin. In his righteous wrath against the man's evil deeds, he included the doer of them, and cursed both together. It should also be remembered that, according to the Oriental style of declamation, the maledictions pronounced on the progenitors and descendants of his enemy are not to be interpreted with the strict literalness which we should apply to a European composition. If it be asked, What then becomes of the Inspiration of the Psalm? we reply, It is indeed inconceivable that God in a mechanical way made the pen of the psalmist write these words; but the real inspiration, the working of God's Spirit in the writer's heart, is clearly visible, both in his righteous indignation against sin, and in the sublime confidence with which in the closing verses he commits his cause to the righteous God—the loving trustfulness with which, helpless and oppressed, he casts himself with all his cares into the Everlasting Arms. We have purposely taken this psalm as the strongest example of its class, and we may recognize the Divine wisdom that has included them in the inspired volume, in order that we may see how by gradual steps God has led our race onwards, how "the glory" of the new covenant "excelleth" that of the old, how "the least in the kingdom of Christ" is in point of enlightenment and fulness of revelation greater than the greatest of the Old Testament prophets.

(vii) The same two considerations which have helped us through the last difficulty, will help us through the next. We find in the Old Testament, *descriptions of God*, which make us wonder. Sometimes God is spoken of as though possessed with the bodily attributes of humanity, sometimes as the subject of human emotions, passions, and infirmities. (The former mode of speech is technically termed *anthropomorphism*, from *anthropos*, man, and *morphos*, form; the latter, *anthropopathism*, from *pathos*, feeling or suffering.) Thus we read of Him as having "back parts" and "front parts," as "coming down" to view the sons of men; again, as being "grieved at the heart;" as being "filled with fury" and "coming out of His place to take vengeance," and anon as "repenting Himself." This language is found almost exclusively in the Old Testament. It is to be attributed partly to the fact, already mentioned, that the earlier conceptions of God were really lower than those we now have of Him; partly to the style of oriental imagery, which employed bolder figures of speech than those which a European writer would adopt. Thus when we read, "He rode upon a cherub and did fly, yea He did fly upon the wings of the wind," this is evidently only a poetic description of the power of God manifested in the thunder-cloud and the storm; or when we read, "He shall cover thee with His feathers, and under His wings shalt thou trust," we have the fostering care of God compared to the brooding of a bird over her young—the very figure afterwards employed by Christ Himself, "Even as a hen gathereth her chickens under her wings," etc. Nor are we to discard as false or meaningless those other expressions which attribute human passions to the Deity. They are not literally correct, but they convey truth in a manner adapted to the minds of those to whom they were originally addressed. Thus, when God is spoken of as repenting and changing His mind, it means that the subsequent acts of His providence were such as, if they had proceeded from a man, would indicate a change of mind. So when he deposed Saul and chose David as his successor, it is said, "God repented that He had made him king." But there was no real change of purpose. God had from the first determined to give the people a king after their own heart, and then a king after His own heart. The real unchangeableness of the Divine character is attested even in the adjacent chapter, where Samuel says to Saul, "God is not a man that he should lie, nor the Son of man that he should repent."

(viii.) A difficulty has sometimes been felt in the occurrence of *passages which offend our delicacy of taste*, and which we could hardly read out before any general assembly. Here, again, we must remember the different condition of the people for whom they were first written. They were much less refined, and what offends our ears would not offend theirs. Further, as regards the plain language in which some sins are described, let us remember that such plain language is needed for some people, and that sin is too serious and awful a matter to be allowed to escape rebuke for fear of wounding fastidious sensibilities. Also let it be borne in mind that it is nowhere said or implied that the whole of the Bible was ever intended to be read in public. It has been well remarked that "the topics of the Bible, however painful occasionally, require no apology if they are not wantonly intruded on a promiscuous audience. If the book is to speak to *every man* as well as to all men it must sometimes talk with us as a parent with his child, as a guardian with his ward, as a friend with an erring brother, as a kind physician with his patient: that is, in confidential secrecy. As we are commanded to enter into our chamber for private prayer, and not stand at the corners of streets: so the Bible, which is to be 'the man of our counsel,' will have some things which are intended not for the pulpit or the class-room, but for our ear alone."

We believe that most Scripture difficulties will come under one or other of the above classes We trust some light has been thrown upon them. We do not profess to have fully explained them. So with passages difficult of interpretation. The student may get some help from commentaries, but he need not be surprised if some things remain inexplicable. It need not for a moment shake his faith in the Divine origin of the Bible. Bishop Butler pointed out long ago, *if* the Bible be a revelation from God, it will probably contain things too deep for us to understand; just as the book of nature does. *That*, too, is a revelation of God: it points unmistakably to a mighty wise and benevolent Being as its author, yet it contains many things hard to reconcile with His wisdom and benevolence. We are content to leave *those* problems only partially solved, saying, "God is great, I know Him not." If the Bible be another revelation from God, it need not surprise us if we are sometimes obliged to say the same concerning the difficulties that meet us there.

BOOKS FOR REFERENCE AND FURTHER STUDY.

General.

"Harmony of the Four Gospels," based on Robinson. (With valuable notes.) Religious Tract Society. 75 cts.

"Progress of Doctrine in the New Testament," by T. D. Bernard. Carters. 75 c.

"Normal Class Manual for Bible Teachers," by Alvah Hovey, D.D., and J. M. Gregory, LL.D. Bible and Publication Society.
"Preparing to Teach," by various authors. Presbyterian Board. $1.75.
"Help to the Reading of the Bible," by Nichols. New Edition, $1.00.
"Bible Scholar's Manual," by B. K. Pierce, D.D. 50 cts.

On Eastern Geography and Customs.

"Manual of Bible Geography. A Text Book on Bible History," containing Maps, Plans, Review Charts, &c., by J. L. Hurlbut, D.D. Rand, McNally & Co. $4.50. (Specially valuable to teachers.)
Stanley's "Sinai and Palestine," (for advanced students.) Carters. $2.50.
"The Land and the Book," by Dr. Wm. Thompson. 2 vols., $6.00.
Kitto's "Daily Bible Illustrations." 8 vols. May be had separately. Carters. $1.25 each.
"Chautauqua Text-Books," No. 26. "The Tabernacle," No. 28. "Manners and Customs of Bible Times." 10 cts each.

On Scripture History.

"Class-book of Old Testament History," by Dr. Maclear. Macmillan. $1.10.
"Class-book of New Testament History," including connection of Old and New Testaments. Macmillan. $1.10.
"Students' Old Testament and New Testament History." (Similar books to the above, but more advanced.) Edited by Dr. William Smith. $1.20 each.
"Outline of Bible History." J. F. Hurst, D.D. 50 cts.
"Chronology of Bible History." C. Munger. 50 cts.

On Scripture Difficulties.

"Can we believe in Miracles?" by G. Warrington. 60 cts.
"Reasons for Believing in Christianity," by C. A. Row. Thomas Whittaker. 75 cts.
Haley's "Alleged Discrepancies of the Bible." Draper.*

---

* For any books mentioned in these lists, send orders to the CONGREGATIONAL SUNDAY SCHOOL AND PUBLISHING SOCIETY, corner BEACON AND SOMERSET STREETS, BOSTON.

CHAPTER V.

ON THE MEANS OF RELIGIOUS INSTRUCTION, PUBLIC AND PRIVATE, UNDER THE OLD AND NEW TESTAMENTS, WITH EXAMPLES.

To the thoughtful teacher the question must often have occurred, "How were the people, and, in particular, how were the children, instructed in Divine truth in the days when there were no Sunday schools, no churches, and little or no religious literature?" or, to put the question in other words, By what means were religious knowledge and religious life maintained and diffused during the period covered by the Old and New Testaments? We shall endeavour to answer that question in this chapter. The sources of information are scanty; but there are many suggestive items scattered up and down the Scriptures, which, when brought together and supplemented from other quarters, give us a tolerably complete view of the subject before us.

1. **Parental Instruction.**—This is the oldest, the most natural, the most general, and *may* be made the most efficient means of communicating religious knowledge, and instilling religious principle. No institutions, however useful, however sacred, can take the place of a father's voice and a mother's influence. Throughout the Bible especial stress is laid upon this mode of religious instruction. The God who calls Himself "our Father," and who in His successive revelations to mankind, has all along enforced and continually elevated the sanctity of domestic

life, makes the religious instruction of children a parent's first duty. In the time of the patriarchs, the parent was the *sole* human teacher. It is true we read of a certain Melchizedek, who is called the "priest of the most high God," and who blessed Abraham when returning from his victory over the confederate kings (Gen. xiv.); but his intercourse with the patriarch appears to have been casual, and we have no reason to believe that he discharged the functions of a teacher. The father was at once prophet, priest, and king in his own household; and whatever instruction the later patriarchs gained, beyond that which was communicated to them directly by God, must have been derived from their father Abraham. One of the most touching scenes in the Book of Genesis is where the dying patriarch Jacob gathers his children and grandchildren round his bed, to bestow on them his blessing, to speak to them of their father's God, and tell them what shall be to them in the latter days (Gen. xlviii., xlix.).

When the law was given by Moses, it contained, on the one hand, special injunctions to children to honour and obey their parents, and, on the other, special injunctions to parents to teach their children the ways of the Lord. The Book of the Law was indeed written and laid up in the side of the Ark, but the transmission of its precepts was intrusted chiefly to the devout memories of the people, and the sacred obligations of the parent to his children.* "Therefore shall ye lay up these My words in your heart and in your soul, and bind them for a sign upon your hand, that they may be as frontlets between your eyes.

---

* It should be borne in mind that the powers of memory are much weakened in modern times by continual resort to the aid of writing. Relying upon books to preserve the information we require, the memory is comparatively little exercised. In ancient times long poems and treatises were preserved in the memory, and handed down from generation to generation. We know it was so with the poems of Homer, with the early lyric poems of Britain and Scandinavia, and so, doubtless, it was with many passages of the law.

And ye shall teach them your children, speaking of them when thou sittest in thine house, and when thou walkest by the way, when thou liest down, and when thou risest up. And thou shalt write them upon the door posts of thy house, and upon thy gates" (Deut. xi. 18-20. *Cf.* iv. 9, 10, and vi. 7).

No doubt parents did not all discharge this duty with like faithfulness, but there are many interesting instances of its fulfilment. If Eli and Samuel were wanting in this respect, David, at least in the case of Solomon, appears to have done all that a parent could to instruct and train him aright. Worth pondering are his words, "And thou, Solomon my son, know thou the God of thy father, and serve Him with a perfect heart and with a willing mind: for the Lord searcheth all hearts, and understandeth all imaginations of the thoughts: if thou seek Him, he will be found of thee; but if thou forsake Him, he will cast thee off for ever" (1 Chron. xxviii. 9). Interesting, too, is the reference to a mother's teaching in the preface to Prov. xxxi.: "The words of King Lemuel, the prophecy that his *mother* taught him." In that book, as well as in the Psalms and the prophets, there is frequent allusion to the duty of parental instruction. "The father to the children shall make known Thy truth" (Isa. xxxviii. 19), is an injunction that recurs in many forms. Fresh emphasis was laid upon this duty after the return from the captivity, when the heathen marriages of many of the people had tended to the neglect of it. In the uncanonical literature between the close of the Old Testament and the coming of Christ, we read that it was a father's first duty to make his son "know the law." The Talmud, despite many slighting remarks upon woman, says, "He is best taught who has first learned from his mother." But the duty of instructing the child in the law was laid chiefly on the father. "Blessed," said the rabbis, "is the son who has studied with his father; and blessed is the father who has taught his son." Josephus says, " Our honour and the highest end of life is the education of our children, and the observance of the law."

Our blessed Lord himself probably received His first religious instruction from the lips of Joseph and Mary. The apostles Paul and Peter are alike emphatic in their injunction to parents to "bring up their children in the nurture and admonition of the Lord." And as this is the earliest form of instruction mentioned in the Scriptures, so it is the latest of which we have any special example, viz. in the case of Timothy, whose father was a Greek, but whose "mother was a Jewess and believed." To him Paul's last letter was addressed, and there we find that from a child he had known the Holy Scriptures, and when we read in the same Epistle of "the unfeigned faith which had dwelt first in his grandmother Lois, and then in his mother Eunice," we are in no doubt as to who had led him to the knowledge of them (2 Tim. i. 5; iii. 14, 15; compare Acts xvi. 1).

2. **Instruction by Rites and Symbols.**—We have already (Chap. IV.) called attention to the fact that the Jewish Ritual was a kind of pictorial instruction in religious truth. This form of instruction may be traced back beyond the time of Moses to the patriarchal sacrifices. They were not *simply* an expression of devotion on the part of him who offered them, but also a religious education for those who witnessed them. When the children of the patriarch saw the *best* of the flock and the herd singled out to be offered to the Lord, the lesson was impressed upon them that God must ever be served with the best. When they beheld the struggles and heard the cries of the victim, they were early taught to associate sin with suffering; that "without shedding of blood is no remission." Or if the sacrifice were not expiatory, but a thank offering, they were thereby reminded that all their possessions came to them from God, and that a grateful acknow-

ledgment was due to Him. This symbolic method of instruction was continued and largely developed under the Mosaic dispensation. The sacrifices were classified and systematized, and a special set of men set apart to offer them. Besides the sacrifices, an elaborate ritual, and a code of ceremonial law were provided, which, while in part determined by sanitary considerations, were intended to be morally and spiritually significant. These laws relating to uncleanness, the white raiment of the priests, the inscription on the high priest's mitre, the constant ablutions, the very structure of the sanctuary itself, with its holy place, and its holy of holies, were all so many pictorial lessons on the necessity of purity and holiness. It was God saying over and over again in many forms, "Be ye holy, for I am holy." Many special ceremonies in the Mosaic ritual, such as the anointing with the blood, the observance of the day of atonement, the scapegoat, etc., were designed to impress the same lesson, and to hint at other important truths which were to be further developed in the progress of Divine revelation.

The three great annual feasts of the Passover, the "First fruits" (or Pentecost), and the "Ingathering" (or Tabernacles), were also a means of instruction. The two latter, at the seasons of the harvest and the vintage, were a constant reminder to the people that "the earth is the Lord's and the fulness thereof." The last was also commemorative of a great epoch in the nation's history, and the first of the three still more markedly called to mind God's deliverance of the people. In connection with the feast of the passover this injunction was given, "It shall come to pass when your children shall say unto you, 'What mean ye by this service?' that ye shall say, 'It is the sacrifice of the Lord's passover, who passed over the houses of the children of Israel in Egypt when He smote the Egyptians, and delivered our houses.' And thou shalt show thy son in that day, saying, 'This is done because of that which the Lord did unto me when I came forth out of Egypt'" (Ex. xii. 26, 27; xiii. 8). It is true that these great feasts were celebrated with their full ritual only in the city of Jerusalem; but all the male Israelites were directed to come up thither, and they would return to their homes, and tell their children what they had heard and seen.

The institution of the Sabbath scarcely comes under the head of "instruction by rite and symbol," nor does it appear that any distinct provision was made for Sabbath *worship* till the time of the kings or later. But if the day was to be observed as "holy to the Lord," it is probable that some portion of it would be spent in exercises of devotion; and the mere setting apart of the day, week by week, inculcated this two-fold lesson: (1) Time is the Lord's: it is not to be wholly consumed in selfish ends; (2) Thou shalt care for thy manservant and maidservant, and even for thine ox and thine ass, and afford them needful rest.

3. Public Reading of the Scriptures.—To what extent this was done in connection with the ordinary temple service we are not informed. But in Deut. xxxi. 9-13, we have a very express direction on the subject. "And Moses wrote this law and delivered it unto the priests, the sons of Levi, . . . and unto all the elders of Israel. And Moses commanded them saying, At the end of every seven years, in the solemnity of the year of release, in the feast of tabernacles, when all Israel is come to appear before the Lord thy God in the place which He shall choose, thou shalt read this law before Israel in their hearing. Gather the people together, men, and women, and children, and thy stranger that is within thy gates, that they may hear, and that they may learn, and fear the Lord your God, and observe to do all the words of this law: and that thy children, which have not known anything may hear, and learn to fear the Lord your God."

We may infer from several passages in the later writings that this ordinance was not always faithfully observed. In fact, under the degenerate kings of the last period preceding the captivity, there was such neglect of the law that even the temple copy of it appears to have been lost. We read (2 Chron. xxxiv. 14–33) how it was found by Hilkiah the priest, and carried to the king Josiah, who had it read before him, and was greatly distressed to find how its precepts had been neglected and transgressed. "And the king went up into the house of the Lord, . . . and the priests and Levites and all the people, great and small, and he read in their ears all the words of the book of the covenant that was found in the house of the Lord. And the king made a covenant before the Lord, . . . and caused all that were present to stand to it." A still more interesting instance of the Public Reading of the Scriptures in express fulfilment of the injunction of Deuteronomy, is found in the Book of Nehemiah. After the return from the captivity, when Ezra and Nehemiah were labouring to restore the worship and service of God, they summoned the people to a grand observance of the feast of tabernacles. "And all the people gathered themselves together as one man into the street that was before the water gate." There Ezra, from his "pulpit of wood," with the assistance of priests and Levites, read and expounded the law from early morning unto midday. "So they read in the book of the law of God distinctly and gave the sense, and caused them to understand the reading." (The teacher should study the whole of this interesting chapter, Neh. viii.). When the synagogues were established (of which more hereafter) the reading of the law and the prophets formed a part of every service. Nor must we pass over the instructive passage which refers to an earlier period in the reign of Jehoshaphat, where we read that "his heart was lifted up in the ways of the Lord; and he sent to his princes . . . to teach in the cities of Judah, . . . and with them he sent Levites and priest; and *they had the book of the law of the Lord with them*, and went about throughout all the cities of Judah, and taught the people" (2 Chron. xvii. 7–9).

4. **Instruction by Teachers divinely commissioned. The Prophets.**—A prophet is not necessarily one who foretells future events. The word, according to its etymology, means one who "speaks forth" (to the people), one who speaks out (publicly); and in many passages of Scripture "prophesying" is simply equivalent to preaching. It is always implied that the prophet spoke by a Divine impulse. Whether he uttered predictions of the future, or exhortations bearing on the present, it was the spirit of God working within him that moved him to speak. The Hebrew word for prophet comes from a root which signifies bubbling up—gushing forth. A still older name for the prophet was the "seer" (1 Sam. ix. 9), *i.e.* "one who sees," not simply visions and future occurrences, but one who sees God's meaning in the events of Providence, one who sees into the counsels and purposes of the Divine mind. Thus the prophets were the divinely commissioned *teachers* of the Jewish nation, and it is in this aspect that we have to regard them in this chapter. Sometimes they were sent with a special message to individuals, sometimes with more general instruction to the people at large. Moses the first, and in many respects the greatest, of the prophets, appears before us in the more public capacity. His instruction was for all the people. Nathan and Gad, on the other hand, are mentioned in connection with private instruction, in particular with the rebuke and warning given to David after the two great sins of his life (2 Sam. xii., xxiv.); and so with some other prophets who appear just once on the sacred page with their special message to a special person, and after that are heard of no more. More frequently the same prophets appear in both capacities. Thus Samuel has much private instruction

for Saul separately,* but he also harangues the people at large † In like manner Elijah and Isaiah are sent to their respective kings, Ahab and Hezekiah, with special messages from the Lord, but they also speak in the ears of all the people.‡ It may also be pointed out that these special messages to the kings had a bearing on the religious instruction of the people. When the king was induced by the prophet to put down idolatrous worship, and to restore the worship of Jehovah, it was the people who were instructed through the monarch. The later prophets generally appear to have delivered their message publicly, and afterwards to have written it down, either with their own hand or by the hand of their disciples. The thirty-sixth chapter of Jeremiah contains an interesting account of how Baruch wrote down the words of Jeremiah at his dictation (see especially vers. 17, 18), and took the book and read it in the ears of the people, " at the entry of the new gate of the Lord's house."

The teaching of the prophets was in part concerned with future events, and distant nations ; it was in part political, warning the kings against unwise alliances and treacherous advisers; but a large portion of it was personal and practical, directed against such evils as drunkenness, adultery, fornication, undue accumulation of wealth, extortion and oppression, vanity in dress, luxurious self-indulgence, etc., exhorting to repentance, promising forgiveness, and continually denouncing all apostasy from the Lord, and assuring the people that He would be ever faithful to those who loyally trusted Him. Such plain teaching roused up many enemies against them, but in spite of this their influence was great, and by means of

---

* 1 Sam. ix. 25-27 ; xiii. 10-14 ; xv. 13-31.
† 1 Sam. x. 24, 25 ; xii. 1-25.
‡ Compare 1 Kings xvii. 1, xviii. 1, xxi. 17-24, with xviii. 21, etc.; and Isa. xxxvii. 21, xxxviii. 1, xxxix. 3-7, with Isa. i. 10; xl. 1, li. 1, lv. 1, etc. : prophecies evidently addressed to all the people.

their writings it extended over a wider circle than they could reach with their lips.

5. **Schools of the Prophets.** — These institutions deserve separate notice. Their origin is to be traced to Samuel, and we find traces of them down to the time of the first captivity. The first institution of the kind was at Ramah, where Samuel had gathered around him a number of men, who lived together in a group of huts (Naioth) formed of branches of the trees, and gave themselves to the study of Divine truth and the practice of sacred psalmody. They constituted a sort of college or brotherhood, over which Samuel presided, and whom he doubtless employed in the work of instruction. Later on, these institutions increased. In the reign of Ahab we find three comparatively near together—at Bethel (2 Kings ii. 3), Jericho (2 Kings ii. 5), Gilgal (2 Kings iv. 38). The members of them were then called "Sons of the prophets"—not that they were natural descendants of prophets, but had inherited the prophetic spirit, were spiritual children of the prophets. Prophets arose outside of these schools, but not to have belonged to one of them was regarded as a deficiency, and sometimes made a reproach (Amos vii. 12-15). Some were married and some single. The latter lived together and shared one mess (2 Kings iv. 38-44); the former lived in their own dwellings and maintained their own separate households (2 Kings iv. 1-7). The company in each "school" appears to have been very numerous, from fifty to a hundred or more (1 Kings xviii. 4; 2 Kings iv. 43). We once read of four hundred being assembled together, but these were probably from different schools (1 Kings xxii. 6). We know that Elisha, who was at the head of one of these schools, itinerated through the country instructing the people, and we may infer that the men whom he educated did similar work, like those Levites whom Jehoshaphat sent through the cities of Judah; or like the

Norwegian schoolmasters, who, until the comparatively recent establishment of parochial schools, used to travel through the sparse population of Norway from one farmhouse to another, educating the people in their own homes. We may also conclude from the question addressed to the Shunammite woman by her husband—"Wherefore wilt thou go to the prophet to-day, seeing that it is neither new moon nor Sabbath?"—that in connection with these schools of the prophets there was some kind of assembly on the Sabbath days and at the feasts of the New Moon for religious instruction or worship (2 Kings iv. 23; see also vi. 32).

6. **Service of Song.**—Fletcher of Saltoun is credited with the saying, "Give me the making of a nation's songs and I care not who makes its laws." This was an exaggerated way of stating an undoubted truth, that the national songs of any people have a powerful influence on the formation of their character. Now, the national songs of the Jewish people were the Psalms, and such songs as those of Moses (Exod. xv.) and Deborah (Judges v.); all of them bearing a strong religious stamp, and some of them attaining a very high level of spiritual thought. There were, as far as we know, no other lyric poems current in the nation; but the people, as we shall see, were pretty generally conversant with these. They not only formed part of the worship of the temple, but were mingled with their social life and their military exploits. Psalm cxxxvi., with its grand refrain, "O give thanks unto the Lord, for His mercy endureth for ever," was sung before the army of Jehoshaphat when he went to battle; on laying the foundations of the second temple (compare 2 Chron. vii. 6; xx. 21; Ezra iii. 10, 11); and again by the Maccabean army after their great victory over Gorgias (1 Macc. iv. 24). We learn from the Talmud that it was the custom for Jewish families to sing or recite the "Hallel" (Psa. cxiii.–cxviii.) during the paschal meal; and sometimes

"the great Hallel" (Psa. cxx.–cxxxvii.) were sung at the close—this last being probably the "hymn" sung by Jesus and His disciples before they went out to the Mount of Olives (Matt. xxvi. 30). Other Psalms, such as the fifteenth, the forty-eighth, and the eighty-fourth, were sung by the people when they journeyed up to Jerusalem to keep the three great annual feasts; and it is supposed that the one hundred and twenty-seventh Psalm was composed for the sentinels who kept watch over the temple mount.

We have already seen that the cultivation of psalmody was one of the chief occupations of "the schools of the prophets;" but it was carried to its highest perfection in connection with the temple service, the performers being Levites. Of the 38,000 who composed the tribe of Levi in the reign of David, 4000 are said to have been appointed to praise Jehovah with the instruments which David made (1 Chron. xxiii. 5). Over this great body of singers and musicians presided the sons of Asaph, Heman, and Jeduthun, twenty-four in number. Each was the head of a band of twelve, who were what we should call "leaders" in the psalmody, having "scholars" under them. Such a band was attached to each of the twenty-four courses of priests who came up in turn twice a year to minister in the temple service. This would give 288 "leaders," and the remainder of the 4000 (about 166 for each course) would constitute the rank and file or "scholars" of the choir.* Now, these courses of priests and Levites only came up to serve in Jerusalem for a fortnight in each year. During the rest of the twelvemonths they resided in their own homes, and thus we see how a knowledge of the Psalms and of the chants to which they were sung would become diffused throughout the whole land, and be

* See 1 Chron. xxv. It is probable that this elaborate arrangement, though initiated by David, was not fully completed and carried out till a later date.

a powerful educative influence among the people. We know how largely the hymns contribute to the impressiveness of our public worship and the efficiency of our Sunday school work. Perhaps our scholars owe as much to the influence and teaching of the hymns as to the daily lesson; and hence we may estimate the beneficial effect upon the Jewish people produced by their familiarity with such Psalms as the twenty-fifth and the fifty-first, which contain, as it were, the gospel by anticipation; while other Psalms, such as the eighty-eighth and the hundred and thirty-sixth, contain a complete epitome of early Jewish history, a grand rehearsal of the Lord's dealings with His people.

That the psalmody was regarded as a means of instruction, and made subservient to that end, is evident from several passages. In 1 Chron. xxv. 1–8 the choral service is repeatedly called "prophesying," and Heman, one of the leaders of the choir, is called a seer or prophet; and in 2 Chron. xxv. 29 we learn that the choral arrangements were made under the direction of Gad and Nathan, the two chief prophets in the reign of David, though not themselves singers. From these passages we infer that the same Divine influence that inspired the prophet inspired the minstrel, and that the merely pleasurable aim of musical performance was made subordinate to the purpose of edification. Hence we must class the "Service of Song" as among the most important "means of religious instruction."

7. **The Synagogue.** — This Greek word signifies literally "coming together," and was applied first to the *people* who came together, and then to the *building* in which they assembled, just like the words school, college, church. Some such assembling of the people in connection with the schools of the prophets is hinted at, as we have seen, in the time of the kings. But the rise of the Jewish synagogue may more fitly be traced to the time of the exile, when the Jews were cut off from the temple worship,

and whatever other religious ordinances they had enjoyed in their native land. In the Book of Ezekiel, the great prophet of that age, we read repeatedly of the people coming and sitting before him to hear the word of the Lord (Ezek. viii. 1, xiv. 1, xx. 1). "They speak one to another, and say, Come, I pray you, and hear what is the word that cometh forth from the Lord. And they come unto thee as the people cometh, and they sit before thee as My people, and they hear thy words" (xxxiii. 30, 31); and by Jewish commentators the "little sanctuary" spoken of in xi. 16 is supposed to refer to an actual building. After the return from captivity solemn meetings of the people became frequent, and were probably periodic (Ezra viii. 15; Neh. viii. 2; ix. 1; Zech. vii. 5); and during the interval between the Old and New Testaments the synagogue system became fully established. Almost every town and village had its synagogue, not only throughout the land of Palestine, but in all the cities of the Roman Empire where there was a large Jewish population. Where the Jews were not in sufficient numbers to erect and fill a synagogue, they frequently built a *proseucha*, or place of prayer,—a slight structure, often open to the sky, in which devout Jews and proselytes met to worship and perhaps to read (see Acts xvi. 13). In the regular synagogues there was a full Divine service every Sabbath day. A liturgy, or written form of prayer, was used. There were two lessons or readings from Scripture; the first was always taken from "the Law." The Pentateuch was divided into sections in such a way that, reading them continuously from Sabbath to Sabbath, the whole five books of Moses were gone through once in three years.* The second lesson was taken from the second division of the Jewish Canon, "The Prophets."

---

* "Moses hath in every city them that preach him, being read in the synagogues every Sabbath day" (Acts xv. 21).

On special occasions additional lessons were taken from the third division of the Canon, "The Hagiographa, or Holy Writings." Thus, Psalms were read from time to time appropriate to passing events, the great feasts, or the season of the year; and at the feast of Purim the Book of Esther was read, because the feast was instituted in commemoration of the great deliverance of the Jews there recorded. After the reading of the second lesson there followed a sermon, or exposition of scripture. The first lesson was usually read by a functionary specially charged with that duty; but the second lesson and the exposition might be given by any devout person who visited the synagogue. Thus we find that Jesus read the second lesson for the day (which happened to be from Isa. lx.) in the synagogue at Nazareth, and delivered a discourse based upon it (Luke iv. 16, and ff.). He frequently preached in the synagogue at Capernaum, and one of his discourses there is recorded in John vi. (see verse 59). When Paul and Barnabas went into the synagogue at Antioch in Pisidia, they listened to the reading of the two lessons. "And after the reading of the law and the prophets, the rulers of the synagogue sent unto them, saying, Ye men and brethren, if ye have any word of exhortation for the people, say on." Then follows the discourse (Acts xiii. 16–41). Paul made it his practice, in coming to any city with his gospel message, to go first into the synagogue, if there was one, and (availing himself of the privilege accorded to any devout Jew) to stand up and deliver it there (see Acts xvii. 1, 2; xviii. 4, 19; xix. 8, etc.). In this way the scattering of the Jews, and the synagogues which they built in every place, facilitated the progress of the gospel.

8 **Schools.**—Children were *allowed* to attend the synagogue at five or six years old. When a boy reached the age of thirteen, he was *required* to do so, and was thenceforward called a "Son of the Law." The "Sopherim,"

or leaders of the synagogue, also instructed children privately. For the children of the wealthy, schools were to be found in the chief cities at the time of Christ, where what we should call a liberal education was given, embracing Greek, Latin, and other subjects. Josephus tells us that King Herod, when a boy, went to such a school in Jerusalem. But the attempt to establish schools for the lower and middle classes appears to have been only partially successful. The ordinary education of the Jew did not go beyond a knowledge of "the Law;" and for this knowledge, even in later times, he was chiefly dependent upon the instruction of his parents and what he heard in the synagogue. There were, however, attached to some synagogues, chambers in which the children were taught to read and to repeat portions of the law. In the courts of the temple at Jerusalem there was such a chamber, called "the hall of hewn stones," where somewhat fuller instruction was given. It was probably in this chamber that Jesus was found by His parents on the occasion of His first passover: sitting on the ground before the rabbis (as was the manner of Jewish children when in school), "both hearing and asking them questions." To Jesus, the son of Gamaliel, belongs the honour of first establishing an "infant school" in connection with the temple, where the children were admitted at the age of six years. But this was shortly before the destruction of Jerusalem (66 or 67 A.D.), so that his work did not last long; for Jerusalem fell in the year 70.

The Rabbinic Schools were designed for young men who wished to pursue the higher study of the law. They entered a "House of Instruction," kept by some learned rabbi in Galilee or Judea. Paul was in this way a pupil of the great rabbi Gamaliel. Most of the rabbinic teaching was very profitless. The rabbis neglected "the weightier matters of the law;" and devoted themselves to allegorical interpretations of the Old Testament narratives;

to fanciful expositions of the shapes of particular letters; and to the formation of a most elaborate system of petty rules on the most trivial subjects, such as to the particular way in which water was to be poured on the hands in washing, the precise weight that might be carried on the Sabbath without breaking the commandment, etc., etc. It is this kind of teaching against which Christ bitterly inveighs in the twenty-third of Matthew and elsewhere. There was, however, one party or school among the rabbis, to which Gamaliel, Paul's teacher, belonged, who devoted themselves more to real moral and spiritual instruction, to the study of Messianic prophecy, etc. To this school are due some of the really beautiful maxims of the Talmud, of which we give a few specimens :—

"Say little and do much. Not learning, but doing, is the groundwork."

"Say not, When I have leisure I will study; perchance thou mayest not have leisure."

"There are three crowns: of the law, the priesthood, the kingship; but the crown of a good name is greater than them all."

"The reward of good works is like dates: sweet, but ripening late."

"The best preacher is the heart; the best teacher is time; the best book is the world; the best friend is God."

9. **The Christian Church.**—We shall say nothing about the religious instruction given personally by our Blessed Lord during His life on earth, as that stands quite in a class by itself; and the missionary labours of His apostles hardly fall within the scope of our inquiry in the present chapter. But we may fitly bring that inquiry to a close by a glance at the beginnings of that wide system of religious instruction which has grown up in the Christian Church. It is evident that during the lifetime of the apostles it was already customary for Christians to meet together on the first day of the week for breaking of bread and mutual exhortation (see Acts xx. 7; 1 Cor. xvi. 2; Heb. x. 25). After the fall of Jerusalem, the observance of the Sabbath was gradually transferred from the

Saturday to the Sunday, and the form of worship in the Christian Church was modelled after the pattern of the synagogue, as were likewise the first buildings erected for Christian worship.

To the readings from the Old Testament, were added first readings from the Gospels, and afterwards readings from the Epistles. In the earliest period of the history of the Churches, before any fixed order of worship was adopted, the instruction was given in the assembly of the Churches in a somewhat promiscuous manner (see 1 Cor. xiv. 26–40); but from the first the apostles laboured to secure orderly proceedings and systematic instruction. When they had founded a Church, they ordained elders to preside over it, and other officers were afterwards added (see 1 Cor. xii. 28; Eph. iv. 11, 12; 1 Tim. iii. 1, 8; Tit. i. 5). The precise office held by Timothy and Titus is a subject on which commentators are not agreed. But it is evident that they were in some way charged with the oversight of several Churches; and the Epistles written to them abound with directions to secure in all the Churches efficient means of instruction. "Sound doctrine," or, as it might be translated, "wholesome teaching," is insisted on over and over again as being indispensable to the Churches' welfare. In the age following the apostolic, it was the custom to form those who had been baptized into "catechumenical" classes, who went through a long course of instruction before they were admitted to full membership in the Church. And thus we have the germ of the manifold institutions and organizations which, under the guidance of the Holy Spirit, grew up in the Christian Church for the education of her disciples in the faith; of which our Sunday schools are a more recent development.

The following extract from the first "Apology" of Justin Martyr, about A.D. 140, will be read with interest, and may fitly conclude this chapter: "On the day called Sunday all who live in cities or in the country gather together into one place, and the memoirs of the apostles or the writings of the prophets are read, as long as time permits ; then, when the reader has ceased, the president verbally instructs, and exhorts to the imitation of these good things. Then we all rise together and pray ; and when our prayer is ended, bread and wine are brought; and the president, in like manner, offers prayers and thanksgivings according to his ability, and the people assent, saying, 'Amen.' And there is a distribution to each, and a participation of that over which thanks have been given, and to those who are absent a portion is sent by the deacons. And they who are well-to-do and willing, give what each thinks fit ; and what is collected is deposited with the president, who succours the orphans and those who through sickness or any other cause are in want, and those who are in bonds, and the strangers sojourning amongst us, and, in a word, takes care of all who are in need."

WORKS FOR FURTHER STUDY AND REFERENCE.

Articles "Prophet," "Music," and "Synagogue," in the Cyclopædias before quoted.

Stanley's "Jewish Church," particularly vol. i. lect. 19, "On the History of the Prophetical Order."

CHAPTER VI.

ON THE TEACHING PROCESS, AS EXEMPLIFIED IN THE BIBLE IN QUESTIONING, METAPHOR AND SIMILE, OBJECT ILLUSTRATION, PARABLE, AND PRACTICAL APPLICATION.

THE Bible was not designed specially to teach the "teaching process." That is an art which, like all other arts, must be acquired by practice, and by a diligent use of all the means which Providence has placed within our reach, in particular by a study of the best models, the methods pursued by the most successful teachers. Such models, however, are placed before us in the Bible. The prophets were great teachers; the Apostle Paul was a great teacher; Jesus Christ was *the* Great Teacher. From the study of their teaching, so far as it is recorded on the page of Scripture, we may gather many useful hints. The object of this chapter is simply to call attention to the five elements of effective teaching enumerated in the title as exemplified in the teaching of Holy Writ.

1. **Questioning** may be employed by the teacher in three ways. It may be used simply to discover to the pupil his own ignorance. Questions may be asked as an *introduction* to the subject (even though the teacher may know his pupil cannot answer them), in order to remind him of what he does not know, and awaken the desire for knowledge. Or they may be asked at the *close* of instruction, as a means of recalling and impressing on the pupil's memory what he has been taught. Or, again, they may be employed

in the course of instruction, to set the pupil thinking, to draw out his powers of observation and reflection, and to lead him, by applying the truth already in his possession, to reach forth to, and infer, other truths hitherto unperceived by him.* This last is the highest form of the art of questioning, and the illustrations which we shall give from the Bible will be chiefly of this kind. If the conversations and discourses of the great teachers of Scripture were reported at full length, we should probably have instances of whole *series* of questions so framed as to lead the person addressed on from one point to another, bringing out by degrees the ultimate truth aimed at. But the Scripture narrative supplies us, for the most part, with only condensed accounts of these discourses, in which a simple question is made to serve this purpose. Thus, when the Pharisees asked Christ whether it were lawful to pay tribute to Cæsar or not (Matt. xxii 17); if He said "No," they were ready to accuse Him to the Roman authorities, as exciting the people to insubordination and revolt; if He said "Yes," they would represent Him to the people as being willingly subservient to the heathen invader, and no true defender of God's heritage But Christ said, "Show me the tribute money," and then asked, "*Whose image and superscription is this?*" They were compelled to answer, "Cæsar's," and thus brought to see and acknowledge that, since the coin of the realm bore Cæsar's stamp, he was their lawful governor in things temporal. And the way

---

* Questions may also be employed in the course of instruction simply to rouse flagging attention. This is, of course, quite a subordinate use of questions, but sometimes very useful. When drowsiness or listlessness is stealing over a class, the teacher may sometimes banish it by pausing in the course of his exposition or exhortation, and firing a few rapid shots, passing the questions on from scholar to scholar, till attention is thoroughly aroused. He may put just what he is going to say in the form of a question, and if questions of the first and third kind do not occur to his mind at the moment, he can always fall back upon the second, and question them upon what he has been teaching.

was paved for Christ's further answer, "Render, therefore, unto Cæsar the things that are Cæsar's, and to God the things that are God's." In the case of the lawyer, however (Luke x. 25–37), we have a succession of at least two questions. The lawyer asks, "What good thing shall I do to inherit eternal life?" Jesus rejoins with the question, "What is written in the law? how readest thou?" The lawyer answers, "Thou shalt love the Lord thy God with all thy heart, and thy neighbour as thyself." Well, says Christ, "This do and thou shalt live." He knew that the lawyer had not kept the law perfectly. Even if he had kept the *letter*, he had broken the *spirit* of it; but Jesus would not *tell* him so; He wished to make him find it out for himself. The lawyer, anxious to justify himself, asks, "Who is my neighbour?" Jesus, in reply, tells the story of the Good Samaritan, and then puts another question, "Which of these three, thinkest thou, was neighbour to him that fell among thieves?" The lawyer answers, "He that showed mercy on him." He is made to feel that he had taken the word "neighbour" in too narrow a sense; that the bitter hatred which he and his class cherished against the Samaritans was against the spirit of the law; and that, if he would really keep it, he must show mercy to all who were in need, of whatsoever race or creed: and he is made to see this by means of *questions*.

Similarly, in the case of Simon (Luke vii. 36–50), Jesus first tells the parable of the debtor who was forgiven the five hundred pence, and the debtor who was forgiven the debt of fifty, and then asks, "Tell Me, Simon, which of them will love him most?" So bringing home to his heart the consciousness that he loved Christ little because he felt little need of forgiveness. Again, in the parable of the wicked husbandmen (Matt. xxi. 40), the guilt of the Jews and the fact that they really deserved their impending doom, is brought home to them by the question, "When the lord therefore of the vineyard cometh, what will he do unto those husbandmen?" They must needs answer, "He will miserably destroy those wicked men, and let out his vineyard to others who shall render him the fruits in their seasons." The question addressed to the young ruler, "Why callest thou Me good?" was doubtless designed to make him think. So, likewise, the double question to the Pharisees (Matt. xxii. 41-45), "What think ye of Christ? Whose Son is He?" "They say unto Him, 'The Son of David.'" Good! the answer is so far right; but Jesus follows it up with another question: "How, then, doth David in spirit call Him Lord, saying, 'The Lord said unto my Lord,' etc.? If David, then, called Him Lord, how is He his Son?" Thus, by a series of questions, Christ leads them on to think and discover for themselves that the promised Messiah must be more than they had anticipated—more than a great prophet, or a conquering prince—that He must be in a very real sense Divine.

2. **Metaphor and Simile.**—A *Simile*, or similitude (Lat. *similis*, "like," *similitudo*, "likeness"), is a figure of speech in which a likeness is traced between the qualities or behaviour of two different objects; *e.g.* "Like as a father pitieth his children, so the Lord pitieth them that fear Him;" "The sun is as a bridegroom coming out of his chamber, and rejoiceth as a strong man to run a race." A *Metaphor* (Gr. *metaphero*, "I transfer") is a figure of speech in which some quality or attribute of one object is transferred to another object, on account of some resemblance between the quality or attribute so tranferred to some quality or attribute of the object to which it is transferred. Hence a metaphor is a condensed simile—a simile in which the comparison is suggested or implied without being stated. Thus, when Milton speaks of "the golden-tressed sun" it is a metaphor. If he had said, "The bright rays of the sun are like the golden tresses of a maiden's head," it would have been a simile. What is required in metaphors and similes is that they should be sufficiently

obvious, and that the things introduced for the sake of comparison should be such as are familiar to the hearer or reader. We sometimes meet with metaphorical language in the Bible which is not very clear to us, because it is based on some Oriental practice or circumstance which does not occur in our own time and country; but they would be perfectly well understood by the people to whom they were first spoken. Some instances of this kind have been given in the section on "Figurative Language," Chap III. Again, when the prophet encourages us to do good and spread the truth in every place, saying, "Blessed are ye that sow beside all waters, that send forth thither the feet of the ox and of the ass" (Isa. xxxii. 20), we need the information, in order to appreciate this figure, that in Palestine and Egypt almost the only ground suitable for corn-growing lay along the banks of the rivers, whence it could be easily supplied with water; and that oxen and asses were employed in ploughing the ground. Even our Lord's beautiful comparison of Himself to the good shepherd who lays down his life for the sheep, while the hireling flees at sight of the wolves, though we understand it, does not come home to us with the force it would do to Christ's hearers, who lived in a place and time where such incidents were of frequent occurrence. The Sunday school teacher, in framing his own illustrations, should be careful that they are such as his scholars can readily understand, drawn as far as possible from the circumstances of their own life. Otherwise he will only obscure his teaching instead of making it plainer.

Most of the metaphors and similes of Scripture are adapted to all times and countries, many of them being drawn from the phenomena of the sky, and others from the most necessary operations and relationships of human life. And there is such an abundance of them that it is difficult to select specimens. We may, however, call attention to the exceeding beauty of the simile used by Moses to set forth the gentle nature and the refreshing quickening power of the Divine word, when he says, "My doctrine shall drop as the rain; my speech shall distil as the dew: as the small rain upon the tender herb, and as the showers upon the grass" (Deut. xxxii. 2). On the other hand, when Jeremiah would describe how that same word *forces* conviction upon the hard and impenitent heart, he writes: "Is not My word like as a fire? said the Lord, and like a hammer that breaketh the rock in pieces" (Jer. xxiii. 29). How graphic are these two similes which follow the one just quoted from the discourse of Moses, employed to set forth God's care of His people Israel! "He kept him *as the apple of His eye*: as an eagle stirreth up her nest, fluttereth over her young, spreadeth abroad her wings, taketh them, beareth them on her wings; so the Lord alone did lead him." How pathetic is the lamentation of Hosea over the faint and fleeting character of any signs of amendment shown by his people in their later days: "O Ephraim, what shall I do unto thee? O Judah, what shall I do unto thee? for your goodness is as a morning cloud, and as the early dew it vanisheth away"! (Hos. vi. 4). On the other hand, "the path of the just is as the shining light (*i.e.* the rising sun), which shineth *more and more* until the perfect day" (*i.e.* high noon) (Prov. iv. 18). Another beautiful simile, drawn from the heavenly bodies, which the Sunday school teacher may take as an encouraging motto for himself, is to be found in Dan. xii. 3 : "They that be wise shall shine as the brightness of the firmament, and they that turn many to righteousness as the stars for ever and ever."

The Apostle Paul frequently borrows images from the Grecian games, with which both he and his readers were well acquainted. "Know ye not that they which run in a race run all, but one receiveth the prize? So run, that ye may obtain. . . . I therefore so run, not as uncertainly; so fight I, not as one that beateth the air: but I keep under my body" (lit. smite it in the face), "and bring it into subjection," etc. (1 Cor. ix. 24–27). Compare Phil. iii. 13, 14, and Heb. xii. 1, 2. We have here a mingling of simile and metaphor. To the class of similes should be reckoned the group of figures at the commencement of Psa. xviii.: "I will love Thee, O Lord, my strength. The Lord is my rock, and my fortress and my deliverer: my God, my strength, in whom I will trust; my buckler, and the horn of my salvation, and my high tower." But the expression, "gird up the loins," to denote moral energy and activity, so frequently employed in the Old and New Testament, is an instance of metaphor. So when Paul speaks of himself as "holding forth the word of life," he is evidently using the metaphor of a lantern which one holds forth to show others the way; the metaphor having been suggested by the one in the preceding verse: "Among whom ye shine as lights in the world" (Phil. ii. 15, 16). "Tossed to and fro, carried about with every wind of doctrine" (Eph. iv. 14), is a very suggestive metaphor. In the Epistle of Jude we have a rapid succession of images used to describe the hypocritical Christians, who beneath an outward profession of religion scarcely concealed the depravity and corruption of their hearts. We quote from the Revised Version. "These are they who are hidden rocks in your love feasts when they feast with you, shepherds that without fear feed themselves, clouds without water carried along by winds, autumn trees without fruit, twice dead, plucked up by the roots, wild waves of the sea foaming out their own shame, wandering stars for whom the blackness of darkness has been reserved for ever." How forcibly do these figures bring out the dangerous influence, the selfish rapacity, the utter barrenness and uselessness, the shameless wantonness, and the eternal doom of these wretched men!

3. **Object Illustration.**—We have already pointed out (Chaps. IV. and V.) how the sacrifices and other portions of the Mosaic ritual were a part of God's "teaching

process" for the Jews. These outward symbols were all of them objective illustrations of spiritual truths. The *prophets* also frequently made use of outward objects to illustrate and enforce their teaching. Thus when Ahab and Jehoshaphat inquired of the prophets whether they should go to war with Syria, Zedekiah, the son of Chenaanah (though he was a false prophet), "made him horns of iron, and said, Thus saith the Lord, With these shalt thou push the Syrians until thou have consumed them" (1 Kings xxii. 11). Zechariah, when he wished to emphasize the fact that the covenant between him and his people was broken, and that the brotherhood between Israel and Judah was finally dissolved, made two staves, one of which he called "Beauty," to signify the covenant, and the other "Bands" (or as it is in the margin, "Binders"), to signify the union between the two kingdoms, and for a time led a flock of sheep with them. Then he cut asunder first the staff "Beauty," and then the staff "Bands," in the sight of all the people, telling them that the covenant and the brotherhood were broken and annulled (Zech. xi. 3–14). Again, when the Lord would impress upon Amos that the time for reckoning with his sinful countrymen had come, and that they were now ripe for destruction, He showed him a basket of ripe summer fruit as an object illustration (Amos viii. 1, 2). Compare with this the two baskets of figs shown to the prophet Jeremiah (Jer. xxiv.); also the "linen girdle" (xiii. 1–11), the "potter's wheel" (xviii. 1–10), and the "yokes" (xxvii. 2; xxviii. 10).

When Ezekiel prophesied among the Jewish captives in Babylon, the exiled inhabitants of *Israel* had been in captivity for more than two hundred years, scattered over various portions of the Old Assyrian Empire, spiritually dead, and as a nation utterly ruined, and as it were buried in heathendom. It seemed impossible that they could ever be revived and restored. So when God would teach His servants that nothing was too hard for His Word and

Spirit to accomplish, and that He would indeed revive and restore these lost sheep of the house of Israel, He led Ezekiel into a valley of dry bones, and bade him prophesy to the four winds of heaven to blow upon them; and the bones came together and stood upon their feet, an exceeding great army. Then the Lord said to the prophet, "Son of man, these bones are the whole house of Israel. Behold they say, 'Our bones are dried, and our hope is lost; we are cut off for our parts.' Therefore prophesy and say unto them, 'Behold, O my people, I will open your graves . . . and put my spirit in you, and ye shall live, and I will place you in your own land'" (Ezek. xxxvii. 1–14). Probably the prophet saw this only in vision; but none the less does it exemplify the principle of object illustrations.

In the examples hitherto quoted, the objects are used as *figures* and *symbols*; but they may be used as direct *examples* for the enforcement and illustration of moral lessons. The ant is so used in the Book of Proverbs, as an example of diligence and providence: "Go to the ant, thou sluggard; consider her ways, and be wise: which having no guide, overseer, or ruler, provideth her meat in the summer, and gathereth her food in the harvest" (Prov. vi. 6–8). And we may remark in passing, that recent observation of the habits of the ant has fully confirmed the accuracy of this description, which was at one time called in question by naturalists. In Prov. xxx. 25–28 the conies (or rabbits), the locusts, and the spider are employed along with the ant to illustrate kindred truths.

Perhaps the most beautiful of all object illustrations are those employed by our Lord, when He makes the lilies growing round Him, and the birds flying above His head, teach His disciples the lesson of confidence in their heavenly Father's care. It is probable, too, that when He uttered the parable of the Sower He pointed to a man actually sowing his seed, a real "object" before His hearers' eyes

These passages are so well known that they need not be quoted. One chief excellence about them is the commonness of the objects, the frequency with which they would present themselves afterwards; and surely the disciples, whenever they looked upon a lily or a raven, or saw a peasant going forth with his seed basket, would recall the words of their Master, and the precious truths contained in them.

If, as is almost certain, the preparations for the passover were actually going on when Paul was writing the First Epistle to the Corinthians, and the Jews were choosing out the paschal lamb, baking their unleavened bread, and sweeping their houses clean, as the custom was at passover time, lest any crumb of leavened bread might linger in the corners and unhallow the feast, then we have an instance of object illustration in his words, "Know ye not that a little leaven leaveneth the whole lump? Purge out therefore the old leaven, that ye may be a new lump, as ye are unleavened. For even Christ our Passover is sacrificed for us: therefore let us keep the feast, not with the old leaven, neither with the leaven of malice and wickedness; but with the unleavened bread of sincerity and truth" (1 Cor. v. 6–8).

4. **Parable.**—A parable (Greek, *parabole*, a putting side by side, a comparison) is a short story in which natural incidents are made suggestive of spiritual truth. If it extends to great length it is called an *Allegory*. It is distinguished from the *Fable*, herein, that the latter embodies rather moral than spiritual truth, and in it inanimate objects, such as beasts, trees, and flowers, are endowed with the powers of human thought and speech. This is not the case with the parable, at least in the more restricted use of the word:* the incidents are all natural.

---

* In a more general sense the word "parable" is applied to any kind of comparison in figurative speech. See Numb. xxxiv. 3–9, Luke vi. 39, etc.

Hence the "parable" of Jotham (Jud. ix. 8–15), the earliest in the Bible, belongs rather to the class of fables. It is very suggestive, well worth study as an example of Oriental figurative speech, but can hardly be said to form part of a "teaching process," so need not detain us here. The same applies to the message which Jehoash, king of Israel, sent to Amaziah, king of Judah (2 Kings xiv. 9).

But we must not pass over the parable of Nathan, which he spoke to David after his adultery with Bathsheba and murder of Uriah (2 Sam. xii. 1–14). There were many points of view from which David's double sin might be regarded. This parable was designed to bring out the utter *selfishness* of his conduct. "There were two men in one city; the one rich, and the other poor. The rich man had exceeding many flocks and herds: but the poor man had nothing save one little ewe lamb, which he had bought and nourished up: and it grew up together with him, and with his children; it did eat of his own meat, and drank of his own cup, and lay in his bosom, and was unto him as a daughter. And there came a traveller unto the rich man, and he spared to take of his own flock and of his own herd, to dress for the wayfaring man that was come unto him, but took the poor man's lamb, and dressed it for the man that was come to him." Here, as in other parables, the *main* features of the story are alone significant. Other parts, such as the coming of the wayfaring man, are introduced simply to make the story more effective, and must not be forced into yielding a spiritual interpretation. But the selfishness and greed of the rich man in robbing the poor man of his one pet lamb, admirably pourtrays David's behaviour in robbing Uriah of his one wife. Most certainly this parable was part of a "teaching process." So pathetic is the tale, that David, supposing it to be fact, is roused to the hottest indignation, and exclaims, "As the Lord liveth, the man that hath done this thing shall surely die;" and when once he recognizes it as a parable, it opens his eyes (which had hitherto been strangely closed) to the baseness of his own conduct; and he cries, "I have sinned against the Lord."

A very beautiful parable is contained in Isa. v. 1–7, where the prophet, under the figure of a vineyard, which in spite of the utmost care and culture brought forth only wild grapes, teaches the men of Judah how little they had profited by all God's training of them, and how richly they deserved the punishment hanging over them. Other instances of teaching by parable in the Old Testament are to be found in Ezek. xvii. 3–10; xix. 2–9; xxiv. 3–5; and to these we might add the parable of the wise woman of Tekoah (2 Sam. xiv. 5–11).

The *parables of our Lord* form one of the most characteristic features of His teaching. So frequent were they in His discourses that it is said, "Without a parable spake He not unto them." Archbishop Trench numbers them at thirty in his exposition. The editor of the "Student's Aids" reckons forty by counting in among them some which should perhaps rather be regarded as similes, such as the New Wine and Old Bottles (Luke v. 37), the Household Watching (Mark xiii. 34, 35), etc. They have been variously classified, on several different principles, such as the periods when they were spoken, the places where they were spoken, the Gospels in which they occur, the truths which they set forth, and the sources from which the illustrations are drawn. The last is a very simple division, viz. into two, the Parables drawn from Nature, and the Parables drawn from the Incidents of Social Life. In both cases the wisdom of Christ is seen in selecting objects and incidents with which His hearers would be familiar— leaven, mustard-seed, tares, a barren fig-tree—a lost sheep, a lost piece of money, a wedding feast, hiring labourers for the vineyard, and so on. The meaning of most of them was very apparent, a few needed special explanation to His disciples. Their value in the teaching process cannot be over estimated. They have always been favourite subjects for pulpit and class instruction; they linger in the memory when other parts of Scripture are forgotten; they have so impressed the heart and laid hold on the imagination that they have given a distinctive sense to the word "talents" in the English language, while "a Good Samaritan" and "a Prodigal" have become proverbial expressions. No eye save God's can count the burning tears of penitence that have dropped upon the page that tells of that poor wanderer's return, or how many hearts it has made to re-echo with the cry, "I, too, will arise and go to my Father."

The discourses of the apostles, as reported in the Acts, do not contain any parables, possibly because they are not fully reported, possibly because the occasions on which they were spoken were not so suitable for this form of teaching. Nor was it likely they would occur in *letters*; but in the fourth chapter of Galatians, Paul nearly approaches the parable, when he makes an allegorical use of the incidents recorded in Gen. xxi. 1-10. The Galatians had been greatly troubled by Judaizing teachers, who persuaded them that they ought to be circumcised and keep the law of Moses as given in Sinai. Paul is anxious to show them that if they did so they would be going backward rather than forward—going back into the bondage of law from the freedom of the gospel. So he reminds them that Abraham had two sons—Ishmael, the son of the bondwoman Hagar, who was born first without any special command or promise of God, in a natural way; Isaac, the son of Abraham's true wife, Sarah, the free woman, who was born to him in fulfilment of God's special promise, by Divine intervention. And Ishmael teased and persecuted Isaac, and was in consequence cast out from Abraham's home along with his mother Hagar. Now Paul says in effect, These Jews who are troubling you, are like Ishmael, children of Abraham by mere natural descent, and under bondage to the law, which was imposed on them from Mount Sinai. They vex and persecute you as Ishmael did Isaac, for *you* answer to Isaac, being the offspring of the Christian Church, Christ's bride, the heavenly Jerusalem; you are spiritual children, born into the family of God, not by natural descent, but by the new birth of the Holy Spirit through faith in Jesus Christ. You are free from the law of Mount Sinai; you have never been in subjection to it. Why then should you now give place to these Judaizing teachers, and not rather cast them out from your midst as Abraham did Hagar and Ishmael? (Gal. iv. 21-31; and see also v. 12).

5. **Practical Application.**—The wise teacher will, as a rule, practically apply his subject to the hearts and lives of his hearers, appealing to their consciences, and showing how the subject bears upon their personal needs and duties. This is especially needful for children, who are less able than adults to make the practical application for themselves. Though in the instances of direct instruction given in Scripture the hearers and readers are for the most part grown-up persons, we find many significant examples of this personal application. Many of the parables above referred to are thus applied. Thus, when Nathan's touching parable, of the rich man taking the poor man's lamb, has moved David to indignant condemnation of the culprit, he makes the startling personal application, "*Thou art the man,*" and then goes on to point out in detail the iniquity of his conduct. A still briefer application is made by Christ of the parable of "the Good Samaritan," when He has elicited from the lawyer approval of the Samaritan's chivalrous generosity: "*Go thou, and do likewise.*" Very beautiful is His application of the parable of the Two Debtors, in Luke vii., on the one hand, to the weeping sinner at His feet, and, on the other, still more pointedly,

to His host Simon. For her it is encouragement, for him reproof. Her grateful love is evidence that her great debt, her many sins, have been forgiven her. His cold, discourteous treatment of the Saviour, shows that he has known little or nothing of Divine forgiveness: "To whom little is forgiven the same loveth little." The application of the Sermon on the Mount (Matt. vii. 24–27) is peculiar and interesting. The whole sermon has been practical and personal in an eminent degree. It is almost entirely made up of direct injunctions and prohibitions. There would, therefore, have been no special force in any command, appeal, or entreaty. So, instead of anything of this kind, the practical application is itself a parable; and it is impossible to conceive of anything better calculated to clinch the effect of the whole discourse, and secure a practical result in the lives of the hearers, than the striking contrast between the fate of the two builders. The parable has often been misapplied, as though it were to illustrate the difference between building on Christ, and building on some other foundation. But that was not Christ's intention. It was to illustrate the difference between the hearer who does what he hears, and the hearer who does not. Moreover, Christ intended it as the "practical application" of that particular discourse: "Whosoever heareth *these sayings of Mine*, and *doeth* them, I will liken him unto a wise man," etc. "And every one that heareth *these sayings of Mine*, and *doeth them not*, shall be likened unto a foolish man," etc.

The discourses recorded in the Acts of the Apostles have generally very pointed "practical applications." Thus Peter, on the day of Pentecost, after showing how the prophecies of Scripture were fulfilled in the events of that day, and in the resurrection of Christ, concludes his sermon, saying, "Therefore let all the house of Israel know assuredly, that God hath made that same Jesus, whom *ye* have crucified, both Lord and Christ. . . . *Repent, therefore*, and be baptized every one of you ; . . . for the promise is unto *you*, and to your children," etc. "And with many other words did he exhort, saying, Save yourselves from this untoward generation" (Acts ii. 36-40). Stephen closes his discourse abruptly with a sudden and terrible personal application of it to his judges. He had been tracing the history of the children of Israel, showing how first of all their forefathers persecuted Joseph ; next, how they resisted Moses ; then, how they opposed Aaron ; and he had apparently intended to show how, in the time of the kings, they had turned a deaf ear to the prophets, but he breaks off suddenly at the time of Solomon—perhaps because he saw his judges were paying no attention to him, or because he read in their countenances the determination not to be influenced by anything he said,—and makes this home-thrust, " Ye stiffnecked and uncircumcised in heart and ears, ye do always resist the Holy Ghost : as your forefathers did, so do ye. Which of the prophets have not your fathers persecuted ? and they have slain them which showed before of the coming of the Just One : of whom ye have now been the betrayers and the murderers (Acts vii. 51-53). Other instances of practical application at the end of discourses will be found in Acts xiii. 38-41 ; xvii. 29-31 ; xx. 28-31 ; xxvi. 27-29.

The Epistles supply many examples. We have already remarked that the Epistle to the *Romans* approaches, more nearly than any other portion of Scripture, the form of a systematic theological treatise. But after Paul has unfolded the scheme of salvation through the sacrifice of Jesus Christ, and shown its efficiency both for Jews and Gentiles, in the first eleven chapters, he begins the twelfth thus : " I beseech you *therefore*, brethren, by the mercies of God, that ye present your bodies a living sacrifice, holy, acceptable to God, which is your reasonable service," and goes on to enforce that practical holiness which should follow from the hearty acceptance of God's unspeakable gift. The argument of the first four chapters of *Galatians* is to show that Christ has completely freed us from the yoke of the law, ending with the parable of Sarah and Hagar above quoted. Then in the fifth chapter comes the "practical application:" "Stand fast therefore in the liberty wherewith Christ has made us free, and be not entangled again in the yoke of bondage." The First Epistle to the *Thessalonians* dwells much on the second advent of Christ, and the possibility of its coming very speedily and suddenly. Then in the fifth chapter, Paul practically applies this truth, "Therefore let us not sleep, as do others; but let us watch and be sober" (ver. 6); and the rest of the chapter is occupied with exhortations to such behaviour as beseems those who think their Lord may come at any moment. The main argument of the Epistle to the *Hebrews* is that the old covenant made through Moses has been superseded by the new and better covenant made in Christ; and the priesthood of the sons of Aaron has given place to the higher priesthood of Christ. The law was but "a shadow of good things to come." It has passed away, but the glorious Reality has come in its place, to abide for ever. Then comes the practical application, very beautiful, but very solemn. It is twofold: First, Avail yourselves of the privileges of the new covenant with happy confidence—"Having therefore, brethren, boldness to enter into the holiest by the blood of Jesus, by a new and living way, which He hath consecrated . . . let us draw near with a true heart in full assurance of faith," etc. (x. 19–23). Secondly, Beware of backsliding, for Christ is God's *final* provision to meet the sinner's need; and if that prove of no avail to rescue you from the dominion of sin, there is no other sacrifice in store; and the punishment will be great, in proportion to the greatness of the privileges you have abused. "There remaineth no more sacrifice for sin," etc. (vers. 24–31).

Again, the teaching of the eleventh chapter is very beautifully applied in the twelfth. The eleventh chapter enumerates the long list of worthies who have loyally trusted in God, and been upheld by Him in all their tribulations. Yet the course they ran was only a preparation for the Higher Way laid open in Christ, and now the writer conceives them as a great cloud of spectators encircling the course we have to run, as the spectators encircled the racecourse in the old Grecian games, and so makes his practical application, viz. that we should run well: "*Wherefore, seeing we are compassed about with so great a cloud of witnesses*, let us lay aside every weight, and the sin that doth so easily beset us, and *let us run with patience* the race set before us" (Heb. xii. 1).

The reader may discover for himself many other instances in the Epistles; one more only we will note, and have reserved till last, because it is a " practical application " which Sunday school teachers themselves may take to heart, and which may appropriately be cited as our parting word to them. It is the use which Paul makes of his grand argument in 1 Cor. xv. Some persons at Corinth had questioned the reality of the resurrection of believers. Paul, in reply, first establishes by abundant testimony the reality of *Christ's* resurrection; he then shows how the resurrection of Christ's people is bound up with that of their Lord; replies to the cavils of the sceptic, based on ignorance; and points out how vain and futile a thing all Christian labour would be, if its results were to vanish at death. But it is not so. The souls for whom we labour are immortal souls. *The Christian worker works for eternity.* Then comes the glowing description of the glories of the resurrection, too familiar to need quoting; and then this practical application, "*Therefore,* my beloved brethren, be ye steadfast, unmovable, always abounding in the work of the Lord, *forasmuch as ye know that your labour is not in vain in the Lord.*"

BOOKS FOR REFERENCE AND FURTHER STUDY.

"The Teacher's Model, and the Model Teacher." W. H. Groser. Sunday School Union. 50 cents.
"Notes on the Parables," by Archbishop Trench. Appleton. $1.25.
"The Parables of our Lord," by Rev. William Arnot. Nelson. $1.75.
"Laws from Heaven for Life on Earth. Discourses on Proverbs," by **Rev. William Arnot.** Nelson. $1.75.

APPENDIX.

NOTE A. See p. 2.

ON THE EVIDENCE FOR THE AUTHENTICITY AND GENUINENESS OF THE NEW TESTAMENT SCRIPTURES AS COMPARED WITH THAT FOR OTHER ANCIENT WRITINGS.

No precise definition of the terms Authenticity and Genuineness has been given in the body of this work. The fact is they are used differently by different writers. Bishop Watson says, "A *genuine* book is that which is written by the person whose name it bears as the author of it. An *authentic* book is that which relates matters of fact as they really happened." According to this definition *genuine* is the opposite of *spurious*, and *authentic* is the opposite of *fictitious* or fabled. Thus we should say the Gospel according to John is both genuine and authentic. It was really written by John, and the events related in it really happened. The so-called "Gospel according to Nicodemus" is not genuine, but spurious. It was not written (as it pretends to be) by Nicodemus, but by some one who lived several centuries later. Neither is it authentic, for it contains many incredibly absurd stories about Christ. "Gulliver's Travels" is a genuine book, but it is not authentic history. It was really written by its reputed author, Dean Swift; but the persons, places and events described in it are imaginary. Lilliput and Brobdignag are inventions of the author's brain. Many modern writers follow Bishop Watson in their use of these words. But some employ them differently. By *authentic* they mean what

Watson means by *genuine—i.e.* that the reputed author is the real author: and they reserve the word *genuine* for another purpose. They use it as the opposite of *adulterated* or *corrupt*. Many ancient manuscripts have been intentionally falsified. Passages which were deemed objectionable by the copyist have been struck out, and other passages inserted more in accordance with his views. Other manuscripts have suffered grievously through the carelessness of the copyist. Passages have been inadvertently omitted, and sometimes a note written by a later hand on the margin has been copied into the body of the text. A perfectly genuine manuscript or book (in this sense) is one which has come down to us free from these corruptions, precisely as it left the author's hands.

Now, in whichever sense we use the word, we are justified in our statement that the evidence for the authenticity and genuineness of the principal books of the New Testament is stronger than that for the great works of classical antiquity.

1. As to the evidence that the New Testament Scriptures are authentic in the sense of being *reliable history*, "relating matters of fact as they really happened." As we have seen, the various evangelists and apostles support and corroborate each other in their statements as to the origin and early days of Christianity, just as Livy and Tacitus do in relating the history of Rome, only more fully and with fewer discrepancies. For no period of Roman history have we the consensus of so many independent witnesses as we have for the events of the first fifty years of the Church's history. Further be it observed that the allusions in the New Testament history to persons (such as Augustus, Herod, Pilate, Felix, Drusilla, etc.) that figure in the Roman annals are confirmed by classical historians. Moreover, the scanty notices of early Christianity in the classical writers, such as the oft-quoted passage in Tacitus, and Pliny's letter to the Emperor Trajan, agree with the statements of evangelists and apostles.*
And then again, the writers of the New Testament lived far nearer to the events which they record than did the classical historians to most of the events related in their works.

2. As regards authenticity in the sense of *authorship*. For no

---

* See Kennedy's "Popular Handbook of Christian Evidences," Part II., chap. i.

classical works can such a chain of testimony be produced as that which certifies that the earlier Epistles of the New Testament were written by Paul, and the fourth Gospel by John; and, in general, that the books of the New Testament emanated from the apostolic circle, and were from the first received by the Church as apostolic works. The evidence for the seven books that are, by comparison, of doubtful authorship, stands at least on a par with that for the Greek classics, while that for the others is incomparably greater. The references of the classic historians to one another are meagre and uncertain. They seldom or never quote a passage verbally. But we find the writings of the apostles specifically quoted (frequently with the author's name), by a chain of writers beginning with the contemporaries of the apostles themselves, and increasing in breadth as ecclesiastical literature became more abundant.* "In not less than one hundred and eighty ecclesiastical writers (whose works are still extant) are quotations from the New Testament introduced; and so numerous are they, that from the works of those who flourished before the seventh century the whole text of the New Testament might have been recovered even if the originals had since perished." This statement is made on the authority of Dr. Angus.† But the experiment was tried by Dr. Bentley (even more famous as a classical scholar than a biblical critic) and he confirms it. This large quotation of the Scriptures by early writers has an important bearing on our next point, while the evidence for the latter indirectly confirms that for their authenticity.

3. Evidence for the genuineness, i.e. *integrity*, of the New Testament Scriptures as compared with that for the Greek and Latin classics. This depends largely, though not entirely, on the number and antiquity of the manuscripts. It will be understood that neither in the case of the classics nor the New Testament has any manuscript actually written by the author's own hand survived the ravages of time. The oldest existing manuscripts date from the fourth century. This being so, it is evident that it is very advantageous to have a number of ancient manuscripts of the same work to compare together. *All* are but

---

* See the table, p. 33.
† See his "Bible Handbook," p. 7.

copies; but by comparing them, and observing where they agree and where they differ among themselves, we may conclude with more or less certainty what the original was. Thus, if on comparing ten manuscripts of a certain book we found that a certain passage or word was wanting in eight of them, and only found in two, we should conclude that it was no part of the original, but had been inserted later, especially if the eight manuscripts were older than the two. Or supposing that the eight had it, and the two had it not, we should conclude that it did belong to the original, and had been omitted from carelessness or some other cause. The comparison of manuscripts with a view to determine the pure original text has been elaborated into a complete science, with certain fixed regulative principles, by the labour of critics during the last century. Into these principles we cannot now enter, but enough has been said to show the advantage of having a large number of manuscripts to compare; and, of course, the older the manuscript, *i.e.* the nearer it comes to the age in which the writer lived, the less likelihood there is of its having been corrupted.

Now, the *best* editions of the classics have been compiled from only about a dozen or a score of manuscripts, and those mostly of a comparatively recent date. Of Herodotus only fifteen manuscripts are known to exist—the *oldest* being of the tenth century. *One* manuscript of Virgil is said to be of the fourth century, but by *far the greater number* are between the tenth and fifteenth. Drakenborch, in preparing his celebrated edition of Livy, consulted seventeen manuscripts for the first ten books, fewer for the later ones. For the Vipont edition of Tacitus twenty-seven manuscripts were consulted. For Cicero's works about the same number prior to the issue of Orelli's edition. He mentions *three* additional ones that he had collated, and lays stress upon the Turin manuscript of the twelfth or thirteenth century as being of great value.

Now, for the later critical editions of the New Testament upwards of **600** manuscripts have been consulted, most of them dating earlier than the thirteenth century. Full particulars of them are given in the *apparatus criticus* of Alford's Greek Testament. Two of them belong to the fourth century, three to the fifth, six to the sixth; and so on till in the tenth and eleventh centuries they are reckoned by the hundred. And while writing this little work, information has just come to hand of about two hundred manuscripts of the whole or part of the New Testament discovered in the Vatican Library which have not yet been inspected. The New Testament, then, has an enormous advantage over the classics in respect to the number and antiquity of the manuscripts.

But this is not the only advantage. There are the *versions* or *translations;* the Old Latin and the Old Syriac, made in the second century; the Sahidic Egyptian Version, in the third; the Coptic, the Æthiopic, and the Gothic, in the fourth; the Armenian and others, in the fifth. Now, though the actual parchment on which these translations are written is in no case older than the fourth or fifth centuries; yet it is evident they not only supply valuable evidence of the extreme antiquity and authority of the original Scriptures, but also give important aid in determining what is the genuine text : *e.g.* if a certain passage is found in the Old Syriac, it shows it must have been in the copy from which the translation was made ; *i.e.* that it is at least as old as the second century. But to the strong testimony of this array of early versions there is no parallel in the case of classics. We might further note that the veneration with which the books of the New Testament were regarded by the copyists would tend to make them more careful than the transcribers of the classics.

The result of these manifold advantages is just what we might have expected. We can determine the genuine text of the New Testament with much greater certainty than that of any classical work. In nearly all the ancient classics there are passages which are, as the editors say, "hopelessly corrupt ; " *i.e.* the words have been so altered and confused in the copying, that it is no longer possible to guess what the original writing was, or to make any sense of the passage at all. There is not one such instance in the whole of the New Testament.* No doubt, the vast mass of manuscripts that have been examined present a large number of minute variations, in particular words and phrases ; but the art of textual criticism has now enabled us, in most cases, to pronounce with certainty which of the various readings represents the genuine original text; and the remark-

---

* The verse, John v. 4, with the latter part of 3, forms no exception, for it is undoubtedly a congeries of later additions, and in the Revised Version has been removed from the text.

able circumstance is, that, with the exception of the last twelve verses of the Gospel according to Mark, and the first eleven verses of the eighth chapter of John (enclosed in brackets in the Revised Version), there is no passage of any length concerning which any doubt exists as to whether it was a part of the original Scripture or not. The large number of manuscripts, and the different versions, disclose no omissions and no additions of any importance. Compare with this the state of the case with regard to the "Letters of Ignatius." There are fifteen letters in the Latin version and only twelve in the Greek. Each of these versions exists in two forms. Both in the Latin and the Greek, one set of manuscripts contains a shorter form, one a longer. It was long disputed which was the genuine one. But recently an Old Syriac version of the same work has been found; and, behold, there are only *three* letters, and each of these is much shorter than either of the versions in the classical languages! It is by such a contrast that we learn to value the certainty of genuineness afforded by the agreement of all the versions of the New Testament Scriptures.

NOTE B. See p. 32.

ON THE INFLUENCE OF THE PERSECUTION BY DIOCLETIAN IN FIXING THE NEW TESTAMENT CANON.

THE Emperor Diocletian began his reign A.D. 284. The Christians had then enjoyed a long period of repose; but Hierocles, the proconsul of Bithynia, instigated this emperor to issue a new edict of persecution (A.D. 303), which enjoined that the churches should be razed and the "Scriptures" consumed by fire. Many Christian teachers suffered martyrdom sooner than deliver up the sacred books. But others yielded to the influence of terror; and some evaded the law by giving up, instead of the Canonical Scriptures, other Christian books of heretical or spurious authorship. Those persons who delivered up the writings were called "*traditors*" (= traitors; lit. "those who deliver up or betray"), and were severely censured by their brethren. Their conduct led to a schism in the Church. The majority treated the offenders somewhat leniently, and received them back into communion on profession of repentance, but a minority refused to acknowledge them, or any one whom they ordained. This minority, led by Donatus, an African bishop, formed a sect called the Donatists, which existed separate from the Catholic Church four hundred years.

The controversy between the two parties subsequently branched out into other matters; but the root and spring of it all was the yielding up of the sacred books. In the disputes that arose as to whether any one had really been a "traditor," it had to be settled whether the books he had surrendered were or were not the "Scriptures." Both parties in the Church naturally combined to distinguish the sacred writings from all others. The stricter Christians required clear grounds for visiting the traditors with censure; and the more indulgent ones would be anxious to draw the line somewhere, so as not to compromise their faith or seem indifferent. Augustine says that both parties admitted alike the Canonical Scriptures. These must, in fact, have been pretty well defined beforehand; or else we should not find, as we do, in the account of the trials, such expressions as the "Scriptures of your law," used by the Roman commissioners as a sufficiently descriptive phrase of the books to be delivered up. But this persecution, and the serious schism which rose out of it, emphasized the distinction between the Canonical writings and all others, and elevated the former to a higher degree of importance and sanctity. It was during this period that the term "Canonical Scriptures," as applied to the books of the New Testament, first came into use.

NOTE C. See p. 77.

ON SCRIPTURE CHRONOLOGY.

THE student who wishes to go fully into this difficult subject may refer to the elaborate article "Chronology," in Smith's "Bible Dictionary," to the briefer treatment of it by Dr. Angus in his "Bible Handbook" (pp. 209-219), or to Dr. Green's compact little essay on "The Bases of Scripture Chronology," n the "Aids to Bible Students" (pp. 110–113). But in this place we must be content to direct the teacher's attention to the following facts.

1. Of course the dates given in the marginal or central column of reference Bibles are no part of the original Scripture, but represent the result of calculations of learned men, based on the comparison of the various notes of time in the Scripture narrative with each other, and with information obtained from other sources. These notes of time are very fragmentary, and sometimes capable of more than one interpretation. Consequently the calculations made from them are liable to error.

2. The dates given in Bagster's and most other Bibles are taken from Archbishop Ussher's system of chronology, published in the time of the Commonwealth, and somewhat modified by Bishop Lloyd. The chief rival system is that of Dr. William Hales, published near the commencement of the present century. The former follows the ages of the patriarchs and other data as given in the Hebrew Bible; the latter the numbers as given in the Septuagint Version and Josephus. The former is shorter, making only 4000 years intervene between the creation of Adam and the birth of Christ, while the latter reckons 5407. Hales's system is on many grounds preferable, but probably it also is too short. The "Teacher's" (Variorum) Bible wisely abstains from attempting to fix any dates before the time of Abraham.

3. The widest discrepancies between the conflicting systems of chronology are in the early part of Bible history. From the establishment of the Jewish monarchy onwards they approximate, and in the dates they assign for the destruction of Jerusalem by the Assyrians there is only a difference of two years—Ussher giving 588, and Hales 586 B.C.

The general accuracy of the Scripture Chronology for this period is confirmed by the "Canon of the Kings," preserved in the works of Ptolemy (second century A.D.), and by the monumental inscriptions of Egypt, Persia, and Assyria. From the reign of Solomon onward, the student may use the dates of his reference Bible with the assurance that he is not more than ten or a dozen years from the exact truth either way; and from the downfall of Jerusalem to the close of the Old Testament Canon the limits of error are still smaller.

4. The Chronology of the New Testament presents no serious

difficulties. Some of the principal personages, such as the Herods, Pilate, Felix, Bernice, Drusilla, etc., also figuring in Roman history, we get the date of the most important events fixed with perfect certainty, and have abundant confirmation of the accuracy of the Scripture record. Critics differ as to the precise date of a few of Paul's Epistles, and on some minor details, but the dates of our Lord's birth, baptism, and crucifixion, and the leading events of the Book of Acts, admit of no dispute. The reader is perhaps aware that our present mode of reckoning the date of an event—so many years before Christ (B.C.), or so many years after Christ (A.D.)—was adopted in the sixth century from the calculations of a Roman abbot, Dionysius the Little, who, as is now generally agreed, had fixed the birth of Christ four years too late. So that, paradoxical as it may sound, we must say that Christ was born 4 B.C. ; and the present year (1883 A.D.) is really 1887 years after the birth of Christ.

INDEX.

Acts, contents of the book, 44
——, evidence for its authenticity, 14
Anthropomorphism, 91
Antiochus, persecution under, 28
Apocrypha, 25, 51
Apocryphal Gospels, 19, 52
Application, practical, 127
Augustine quoted, 2

Basilides, 13
Bible, the, a book of human life, 67
——, the, a unique book, 63
—— the, divine origin of, *Introductory Letter* viii.-xiii.
—— history, 77
Buddha, prodigies of, 58

Canon of the Old Testament, 26
—— New Testament, 30
Charteris, Dr., his table of Canonicity, 33
Christ's life sketched in the Epistles, 15
Christ's use of the Old Testament, 21
Chronology of Scripture, 77, 133
Chronicles, Books of, 38
Church life in the Epistles, 68, 69
—— in the days of Justin, 112
Classics, authenticity of the, compared with Scripture, 2, 133
Clement of Alexandria, 13, 34
Clement of Rome, 12, 33
Contradictions of Scripture reconcilable, 86
Corinthian Epistles, evidence for, 7
Councils of Carthage and Laodicea, 32

Deuteronomy, meaning and contents, 36
Difficulties in Scripture, 85
Diocletian, persecution under, 32, 138
Dramatic style of Scripture, 56

Epistles of Paul, their authenticity, 3, 12
—— of Paul, their contents, 45
—— of Peter, 48
——, the Catholic, 47
Exodus, meaning and contents, 36

Feasts, the three great, 99
Figures of Scripture, 58, 117

Galatians, authenticity of, 10
——, contents and character, 45
Genesis, meaning and contents, 35
Gospels, authenticity of, 15
——, the four, compared, 42
——, the Apocryphal, 19, 52

Hagiographa, 28
Hebrews, Epistle to the, 47
History, Jewish, summary of, 77
Huxley, Professor, on the Bible, 64

Illustration by natural objects, 121
Impartiality of Scripture writers, 55
Imprecatory Psalms, 90
Internal evidence for the Old Testament, 20
—— for the Gospels, 17
—— for the Epistles, 3
Irenæus, 13, 18
Isaiah, characteristics of his book, 40

Jamnia, Synod of, 28
Jeremiah, characteristics of his book, etc., 41, 103
Job, Book of, 39
John, Gospel of, 43
——, character of the Apostle, 48
——, Epistles and Apocalypse of, 48
Jones, Sir William, on the Bible, 64
Josephus quoted, 29, 98
Joshua and Judges, 37
Justin Martyr, 18, 112

Kings, Books of, 37
—— of Israel and Judah characterized, 78

Leathes, Dr. Stanley, quoted, 23
Lesson-plan, 84
Leviticus, meaning and contents, 36
Luke, Gospel of, 43, 44

Marcion, 13
Mark, Gospel of, 43
Matthew, Gospel of, 43
Metaphors, teaching by, 117
——, difficult, explained, 59

Object Illustrations, 121
Old Testament Canon, 26
—— quoted in the New, 21
Onesimus, story of, 69

Papias, 17, 33
Parables defined, 123
—— in the Old Testament, 124
—— of our Lord, 125
Parallelism of Hebrew poetry, 61
Parental instruction, 95
Pauline Epistles, internal evidence for, 3
——, external evidence for, 12
Pentateuch, Mosaic origin of, 22
——, place of, in the Canon, 26
——, contents of, 35
Philemon, Epistle to, 69
Plan for reading the Bible, 80

Polycarp, 13
Practical application, 127
Preparation of lesson, 82
Progress of Divine revelation, 70
Prophets, the, a division of the Canon, 23, 27
Prophets, the Greater, 40
——, the Minor, 42
——, the, active life of, 68
——, the, as teachers, 102
——, schools of the, 104
Psalms, their inspiration, 40
——, difficulties in, 89

Questioning in class, 114
—— as employed in Scripture, 115

Reading of the Scriptures in public, 100
Revelation, Book of, 48
Rites and symbols instructive, 98
Romans, Epistle of, internal evidence for the, 5
——, external evidence for the, 13
——, summary of contents, 45

Schools of the prophets, 104
—— of the synagogue and temple, 109
——, Rabbinic, 110
Scott, Sir Walter's dying words, 64
Septuagint, the, 21
Similes in Scripture, 59, 118
Song, service of, 105
Style of Scripture, 50
Synagogue, the great, 28
——, service of the, 108

Talmud, 97, 111
Timothy and Titus, Epistles to, 47

Undesigned coincidences, 5
Unique character of the Bible, 63

Valentinus, 13
Versions, early, of the Scriptures, 13, 21, 137

www.ingramcontent.com/pod-product-compliance
Lightning Source LLC
Chambersburg PA
CBHW030252170426
43202CB00009B/713